GREEK LYRICS

Translated by

Richmond Lattimore

SECOND EDITION

REVISED AND ENLARGED

THE UNIVERSITY OF CHICAGO PRESS

CHICAGO & LONDON

SBN: 226–46943–3 (clothbound); 226–46944–1 (paperbound)

THE UNIVERSITY OF CHICAGO PRESS, CHICAGO 60637
The University of Chicago Press, Ltd., London

PREFACE

TO THE FIRST EDITION

For about a century and a half, roughly from the middle of the seventh century B.C. to the end of the sixth, the dominant form of literature in Greece was the independent short poem. We may call them "lyrics," though to the Greeks themselves this term would have described only those poems which were meant to be sung or chanted to the accompaniment of a lyre. Before this period, or so I think, came the age of epic, culminating in the two great Homeric poems; after it came the perfection of drama and the development of prose, for science, speculation, historical narrative, and persuasion. The lyrics of our period were of the most varied kind. We may find them secular or sacred; provincial or cosmopolitan; personal or objectively public; mere sequences of lines or couplets or elaborate stanzas or strophes; and in various dialects. Yet in a way they have a kind of unity, because of the period in which they belong, because of their relative brevity and self-sufficiency, and because of the shared accident of their destruction. We have manuscripts proper only for Theognis and Pindar, and for Pindar all but the victory odes are fragmentary. For other poets, we have only a collection of quotations from subsequent authors and scraps of papyrus from Alexandrian Egypt—mostly fragments, but sometimes poems quoted or preserved in full. The following lyrics are offered here in translation in the hope that they may give some notion of what this poetry was like.

Some of these translations have appeared previously in the *Hudson Review* and the *Quarterly Review of Literature*.

PREFACE

TO THE SECOND EDITION

In making additions to the first printed edition, I have limited myself to poems or fragments which, taken out of context, can still have enough interest or merit to justify their place and have kept reminding myself that if the selection grows too large, it will lose the value of being a selection. The book is still aimed at students (in the widest sense) of literature who do not know Greek or know only a little. Advanced scholars and experts will read these offerings only for fun, or out of curiosity, or pure kindness, or, perhaps, malice.

The notes, too, have been enlarged, but here again I have avoided detail. There may now be a place in scholarship for a *history* of Greek literature designed for the Greekless reader, and such a history ought to have several chapters on the lyric; but this selection is not meant to be a part of any such book. I hope, though, that it will be useful to add a few comments on the types of poetry that have been lumped together under the comprehensive term "lyric" and to give a geographical sketch, with the help of a map, of the distribution of the poets who have been lumped together under the comprehensive term "Greek."

The chief types follow.

Elegiac couplet.—This was based on the Homeric-Hesiodic hexameter and composed in the Homeric (Ionic-Aeolic) dialect. It was the most popular verse form for poetry that was neither narrative nor dramatic nor choral and covered every kind of subject, public and (more often) personal, sacred and (more often) secular. The short elegiac poem, which is what we mostly mean by *epigram*, continued to be the most persistent single form of Greek poetry down to the end in Roman and Byzantine times.

Represented in Callínus, Archílochus, Tyrtaéus, Mimnérmus, Solon, Phocýlides, Xenóphanes, Theógnis, Early Metrical Inscriptions, Sappho (?), Simónides of Ceos.

Iambic.—This is much like our own blank verse in general effect, though the principle was probably quite different. Greek poets think of iambics in pairs, and the six-beat verse is three pairs, or trimeter. It was originally associated with invective or satirical content, was personal rather than public, and secular rather than sacred. At some date hard to determine precisely, it was adopted by Epichármus of Syracuse and the comic poets of Athens for use in the spoken parts of comedy, and by the Athenian tragic poets for the spoken parts of tragedy.

Represented in Archílochus, Semónides of Amórgos, Hippónax (special variant), Solon.

True lyric.—Lyrics would properly mean songs to be accompanied by the lyre. While there is some overlapping and confusion, it is generally possible to distinguish two main types.

Lyric monody.—This includes poems, mostly short, composed in stanzas, designed for a single singer or to be read. They were mostly secular; when sacred, private; and in the local dialect of the writer. It is not, however, always possible to distinguish between monodic and choral lyric, especially in the form of presentation; and the classification of Corínna as monodic is somewhat arbitrary.

Represented in Sappho, Alcaéus, Anácreon, Praxílla, Anonymous Drinking Songs, Hýbrias, Anonymous Lyrics, Corínna, Simónides of Ceos.

Choral lyric.—This includes poems to be sung by a chorus, and poems made in the *form* of such chorales. They were mostly longer than monodies and were composed in far more elaborate stanzas. They were chiefly sacred and public, or semi-public (hymns, paeans, dithyrambs, maiden-songs, victory odes). Choral lyric is mostly composed in a sort of international literary language in which the predominant dialect is Dorian, as Sparta was the early capital of choral lyric.

Represented in Terpánder, Alcman, Stesíchorus, Íbycus, Simónides of Ceos, Pindar, Bacchýlides.

Birthplaces of poets in this selection:

Asia Minor

Cólophon:	Mimnérmus
	Xenóphanes
Teos:	Anácreon
Éphesos:	Callínus
	Hippónax
Míletus:	Phocýlides

Islands
Antíssa:	Terpánder
Mytiléne:	Sappho
	Alcaéus
Amórgos:	Semónides
Paros:	Archílochus
Ceos:	Simónides
	Bacchýlides
Crete:	Hýbrias (not shown on the map)

Mainland
Thebes:	Pindar
Tánagra:	Corínna
Athens:	Solon
Mégara:	Theógnis
Sícyon:	Praxílla
Sparta:	Tyrtaéus
	Alcman

Italy and Sicily (not shown on the map)
Rhégium:	Íbycus
Hímera:	Stesíchorus

The map of lyric poetry shows that Ionia and the Islands dominated elegy and iambic and that the Dorian and Aeolic communities (Lesbos, Boeotia, Sparta) dominated the true lyric. The surprise, for many, will be the small part played by Athens. Solon, good inscribed epigrams, and the drinking songs give some idea of what was to come. Toward the end of the sixth century, good foreign poets, like Anácreon and Simónides, were attracted there, and Pindar himself got some of his early schooling at Athens. But the greatness of Athens in literature was not established until the fifth century. I emphasize this because Greek literature and Athenian literature are too often spoken of as if they were synonymous terms.

CONCORDANCE

CHIEF TEXTS WITH EDITORS

Bowra, C. M. *Pindari Carmina*. Oxford, 1935.

Diehl, E. *Anthologia Lyrica Graeca*. Vol. 1, 2d. ed., Leipzig, 1936; vol. 2, 1st. ed., 1925.

Edmonds, J. M. *Elegy and Iambus*. Vols. 1 and 2, London and New York, 1931.

———. *Lyra Graeca*. Vols. 1, 2, and 3, 2d. ed., London and New York, 1928.

Friedländer, P., and Hoffleit, H. B. *Epigrammata*. Berkeley and Los Angeles, 1948.

Lobel, E., and Page, D. L. *Poetarum Lesbiorum Fragmenta*. Oxford, 1955.

Murray, G. Appendix (pp. 660–74) to Harrison, J., *Prolegomena to the Study of Greek Religion*. Cambridge, 1903.

Page, D. L. *Alcman: The Partheneion*. Oxford, 1951.

———. *Corinna*. London, 1953.

I have used Diehl as the principal text (but with consultation of other texts) except as follows: for Early Metrical Inscriptions 1–6, Friedländer-Hoffleit; for 7, Murray; for some of Sappho and Alcaéus, Lobel-Page; for Corinna, Page; for Pindar, Bowra; and for Bacchýlides, Edmonds.

Archílochus		Archílochus—*Continued*	
Lattimore	Diehl	Lattimore	Diehl
1	1	11	10
2	2	12	12
3	6	13	13
4	15	14	18
5	16	15	56
6	22	16	25
7	60	17	103
8	7	18	53
9	67	19	54
10	74	20	55

For the names of poets and their provenances, I have used the traditional English (romanized) spelling; elsewhere, I have transliterated the Greek.

TABLE OF CONTENTS

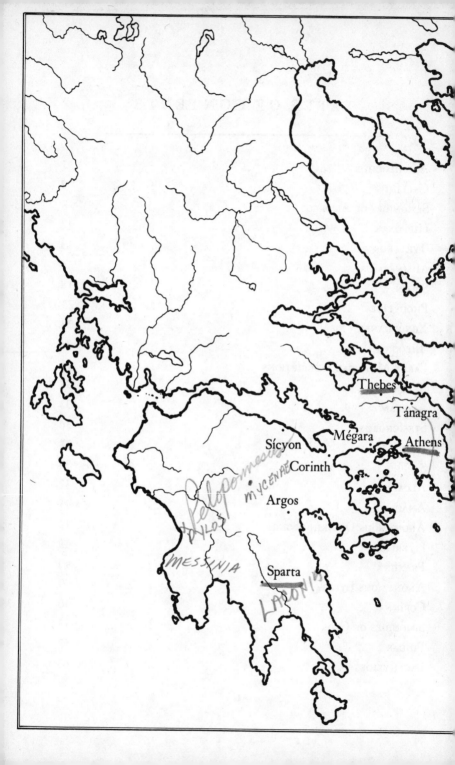

Thebes

Tánagra

Sícyon

Mégara

Athens

Corinth

Argos

Peloponnesus

MYCENAE

PYLOS

MESSINIA

Sparta

LAONIA

Thasos

x TRoy

Antíssa

Lesbos

Mytiléne

IOnia

Attica

Teos

Cólophon

Éphesos

Míletus

os

Paros

Amórgos

ARCHÍLOCHUS

OF PAROS

Archílochus probably lived about 680–640 B.C. A rather short life is suggested by the tradition of his death in battle. Archílochus was the son of a Parian aristocrat and a slave woman. He made his living as a mercenary soldier and took part in the colonization of Thasos, off the Thracian coast, where he fought against the Barbarians of Thrace. The story goes that he was engaged to Neoboúle, the daughter of Lykámbes, but the engagement was broken and Archílochus made the family miserable with his invective. According to one version, the daughters of Lykámbes hanged themselves for chagrin. While this is unlikely, the general account probably contains much truth, since the names of Neoboúle, Lykámbes, and other friends and enemies of the poet appear in his work. It is hard to see how Archílochus could have earned any profitable patronage by the poems he wrote; and he thus stands as one of the earliest known examples, for Western tradition, of the amateur poet, driven by love and compulsion to record his hates, loves, friendships, and amusements. He also wrote beast-fables, apparently of the sort later assembled under the name of Aesop.

The first ten items here given may well be very short complete poems rather than fragments.

EPIGRAMS

· 1 ·

I am two things: a fighter who follows the Master of Battles,
and one who understands the gift of the Muses' love.

· 2 ·

By spear is kneaded the bread I eat, by spear my Ismaric
wine is won, which I drink, leaning upon my spear.

· 3 ·

Some barbarian is waving my shield, since I was obliged to
  leave that perfectly good piece of equipment behind
under a bush. But I got away, so what does it matter?
  Let the shield go; I can buy another one equally good.

4 · *On a Willing Woman*

Wild fig tree of the rocks, so often feeder of ravens,
  Loves-them-all, the seducible, the stranger's delight.

5 · *Epitaph*

O vast earth, you contain Arístophon and Megatímos
  under your folds, the two tall columns of Naxos sustained.

6 · *Charon the Smith*

Nothing to me the life of Gyges and his glut
  of gold. I neither envy nor admire him, as
I watch his life and what he does. I want no pride
  of tyranny; it lies far off from where I look.

tyranny

7 · *Two Captains*

I don't like the towering captain with the spraddly length of leg,
one who swaggers in his lovelocks and cleanshaves beneath the chin.
Give me a man short and squarely set upon his legs, a man
full of heart, not to be shaken from the place he plants his feet.

POEMS

8 · *On Friends Lost at Sea*

Blaming the bitterness of this sorrow, Perikles, no man
  in all our city can take pleasure in festivities:
Such were the men the surf of the roaring sea washed under,
  all of us go with hearts aching against our ribs
for misery. Yet against such grief that is past recovery
  the gods, dear friend, have given us strong endurance to be

our medicine. Such sorrows are variable. They beat now
   against ourselves, and we take the hurt of the bleeding sore.
Tomorrow it will be others who grieve, not we. From now on
   act like a man, and put away these feminine tears.

· 9 ·

Heart, my heart, so battered with misfortune far beyond your strength,
up, and face the men who hate us. Bare your chest to the assault
of the enemy, and fight them off. Stand fast among the beamlike spears.
Give no ground; and if you beat them, do not brag in open show,
nor, if they beat you, run home and lie down on your bed and cry.
Keep some measure in the joy you take in luck, and the degree
you give way to sorrow. All our life is up-and-down like this.

10 · *Eclipse of the Sun*

Nothing will surprise me any more, nor be too wonderful
for belief, now that the lord upon Olympus, father Zeus,
dimmed the daylight and made darkness come upon us in the noon
and the sunshine. So limp terror has descended on mankind.
After this, men can believe in anything. They can expect
anything. Be not astonished any more, although you see
beasts of the dry land exchange with dolphins, and assume their place
in the watery pastures of the sea, and beasts who loved the hills
find the ocean's crashing waters sweeter than the bulk of land.

FRAGMENTS

· 11 ·

I will make nothing better by crying, I will make nothing
   worse by giving myself what entertainment I can.

· 12 ·

Often along the streaming hair of the gray salt water
   they pray for sweet homecoming won in spite of the sea.

· 13 ·

Glaukos, a soldier of fortune's your friend as long as he's fighting.

14 · *Thasos*

Here the island stands
stiff with wild timber like a donkey's bristling back.
This is no place of beauty, not desirable
nor lovely like the plains where the River Siris runs.

· 15 ·

Glaukos, look! The open sea is churning to a wash of waves
deep within. A cloud stands upright over the Gyrean cape,
signal of a storm, and terror rises from the unforeseen.

· 16 ·

Luxurious in a spray of myrtle, she wore too
the glory of the rose upon her, and her hair
was all a darkness on her shoulders and her back.

· 17 ·

The fox knows many tricks, the hedgehog only one.
One good one.

· 18 ·

Say goodbye to Paros, and the figs, and the seafaring life.

19 · *Thasos*

All the griefs of all the Hellenes came together in this place.

20 · *Thasos*

Let not the stone of Tantalos
overhang this island any longer.

· 21 ·

We, a thousand, are the murderers of the seven men who fell
dead. We overtook them with our running feet. . . .

22 · *On Drowned Bodies*

Hide we away these painful gifts of the lord Poseidon.

23 · *The Wreckers and a Former Friend*

. . .

slammed by the surf on the beach
naked at Salmydéssos, where the screw-haired men
of Thrace, taking him in
will entertain him (he will have much to undergo,
chewing on slavery's bread)
stiffened with cold, and loops of seaweed from the slime
tangling his body about,
teeth chattering as he lies in abject helplessness
flat on his face like a dog
beside the beach-break where the waves come shattering in.
And let me be there to watch;
for he did me wrong and set his heel on our good faith,
he who had once been my friend.

· 24 ·

Here I lie mournful with desire,
feeble in bitterness of the pain gods inflicted upon me,
stuck through the bones with love.

· 25 ·

If it only were my fortune just to touch Neoboule's hand.

· 26 ·

Such is the passion for love that has twisted its way beneath
        my heartstrings
and closed deep mist across my eyes
stealing the soft heart from inside my body. . . .

· 27 ·

My lord Apollo, single out the guilty ones;
destroy them, O destroyer god.

28 · *The Fox Appeals for Justice*

O Zeus, our father Zeus, for you control the sky,
you oversee the works of men,
the right acts and the wrong they do; so yours to judge
the crimes and punishment of beasts.

· 29 ·

Father Lykámbes, whatever were you thinking of?
And who seduced the common sense
in which you once were so secure? How things are changed!
Your neighbors giggle in your face.

· 30 ·

To the gods all things are easy. Many times from circumstance
of disaster they set upright those who have been sprawled at length
on the ground, but often again when men stand planted on firm feet,
these same gods will knock them on their backs, and then the
    evils come,
so that a man wanders homeless, destitute, at his wit's end.

· 31 ·

Érxias, where is all this useless army gathering to go?

· 32 ·

No man is respected, no man spoken of, when he is dead
by his townsmen. All of us, when still alive, will cultivate
the live man, and thus the dead will always have the worst of it.

· 33 ·

One main thing I understand,
to come back with deadly evil at the man who does me wrong.

CALLÍNUS
OF ÉPHESOS

Callínus was the contemporary of Archílochus. Little is known about him, except that he encouraged his fellow citizens to resist the invasion of the barbaric Cimmérians. The poem given, which is the only substantial fragment that survives, is concerned with these events.

How long will you lie idle, and when will you find some courage,
    you young men? Have you no shame of what other cities will say,
you who hang back? You think you can sit quiet in peacetime.
    This is not peace, it is war which has engulfed our land.

A man, as he dies, should make one last throw with his spear.
It is a high thing, a bright honor, for a man to do battle
    with the enemy for the sake of his children, and for his land
and his true wife; and death is a thing that will come when the spinning
    Destinies make it come. So a man should go straight on
forward, spear held high, and under his shield the fighting
    strength coiled ready to strike in the first shock of the charge.
When it is ordained that a man shall die, there is no escaping
    death, not even for one descended from deathless gods.
Often a man who has fled from the fight and the clash of the thrown
    spears
    goes his way, and death befalls him in his own house,
and such a man is not loved nor missed for long by his people;
    the great and the small alike mourn when a hero dies.
For all the populace is grieved for the high-hearted warrior
    after his death; while he lives, he is treated as almost divine.
Their eyes gaze on him as if he stood like a bastion before them.
    His actions are like an army's, though he is only one man.

SEMÓNIDES
OF AMÓRGOS

Semónides, the sole literary representative of his little island, was probably at work during the middle or late seventh century. Semónides' second appears to have influenced Solon's first. His work suggests the village sage or cracker-barrel philosopher, but it also constitutes a very early form of satire (as distinguished from the personal invective of Archílochus, Hippónax, Anácreon, Sappho, and Alcaéus). He has, at least, isolated two of the favorite themes of satire, namely, "The Women" and "The Vanity of Human Wishes."

It is altogether doubtful whether Semónides is the right way to spell his name, but it is handy to distinguish between his name and that of Simónides of Ceos.

1 · *An Essay on Women*

In the beginning God made various kinds of women
with various minds. He made one from the hairy sow,
that one whose house is smeared with mud, and all within
lies in dishevelment and rolls along the ground,
while the pig-woman in unlaundered clothing sits
unwashed herself among the dunghills, and grows fat.

God made another woman from the mischievous
vixen, whose mind gets into everything. No act
of wickedness unknown to her; no act of good
either, because the things she says are often bad
but sometimes good. Her temper changes all the time.

One from a bitch, and good-for-nothing like her mother.
She must be in on everything, and hear it all.
Out she goes ranging, poking her nose everywhere
and barking, whether she sees anyone about
or not. Her husband cannot make her stop by threats,
neither when in a rage he knocks her teeth out with
a stone, nor when he reasons with her in soft words,
not even when there's company come, and she's with
        them.
Day in, day out, she keeps that senseless yapping up.

The gods of Olympus made another one of mud
and gave her lame to man. A woman such as this
knows nothing good and nothing bad. Nothing at all.
The only thing she understands is how to eat,
and even if God makes the weather bad, she won't,
though shivering, pull her chair up closer to the fire.

One from the sea. She has two different sorts of mood.
One day she is all smiles and happiness. A man
who comes to visit sees her in the house and says:
"There is no better wife than this one anywhere
in all mankind, nor prettier." Then, another day
there'll be no living with her, you can't get within
sight, or come near her, or she flies into a rage
and holds you at a distance like a bitch with pups,
cantankerous and cross with all the world. It makes
no difference whether they are friends or enemies.
The sea is like that also. Often it lies calm
and innocent and still, the mariner's delight
in summer weather. Then again it will go wild
and turbulent with the thunder of big crashing waves.
This woman's disposition is just like the sea's,
since the sea's temper also changes all the time.

One was a donkey, dusty-gray and obstinate.
It's hard to make her work. You have to curse and tug
to make her do it, but in the end she gets it done
quite well. Then she goes to her corner-crib and eats.
She eats all day, she eats all night, and by the fire
she eats. But when there's a chance to make love, she'll
    take
the first one of her husband's friends who comes along.

One from a weasel—miserable, stinking thing.
There's nothing pretty about her. She has no kind
of charm, no kind of sweetness, and no sex appeal.
She's always crazy to make love and go to bed,
but makes her husband—if she has one—sick, when he
comes near her. And she steals from neighbors. She's
    all bad.
She robs the altar and eats up the sacrifice.

One was begotten from the maned, fastidious mare.
She manages to avoid all housework and the chores
of slaves. She wouldn't touch the mill, or lift a sieve,
or sweep the dung from the house and throw it out of doors,
or kneel by the fire. Afraid the soot will make her dirty.
She makes her husband boon-companion to Hard Times.
She washes the dirt off her body every day
twice at least, three times some days, and anoints herself
with perfume, and forever wears her long hair combed
and shadowed deep with flowers. A woman such as this
makes, to be sure, a lovely wife for someone else
to look at, but her husband finds her an expense
unless he is some baron or a sceptered king
who can indulge his taste for luxuries like her.

One was a monkey; and this is the very worst,
most exquisite disaster Zeus has wished on men.
Hers is the ugliest face of all. When such a woman
walks through the village, everybody turns to laugh.
Her neck's so short that she can scarcely turn her head.
Slab-sided, skinny-legged. Oh, unhappy man
who has to take such a disaster in his arms!
Yet she has understanding of all tricks and turns,
just like a monkey. If they laugh, she doesn't mind.
Don't expect any good work done by her. She thinks
of only one thing, plans for one thing, all day long:
how she can do somebody else the biggest harm.

One from a bee. The man is lucky who gets her.
She is the only one no blame can settle on.
A man's life grows and blossoms underneath her touch.
She loves her husband, he loves her, and they grow old
together, while their glorious children rise to fame.
Among the throngs of other women this one shines
as an example. Heavenly grace surrounds her. She
alone takes no delight in sitting with the rest
when the conversation's about sex. It's wives like this
who are God's gift of happiness to mortal men.
These are the thoughtful wives, in every way the best.

But all those other breeds come to us too from God

and by his will. And they stay with us. They won't go.
For women are the biggest single bad thing Zeus
has made for us. Even when a wife appears to help,
her husband finds out in the end that after all
she didn't. No one day goes by from end to end
enjoyable, when you have spent it with your wife.
She will not stir herself to push the hateful god
Hard Times—that most unwelcome caller—out of doors.
At home, when a man thinks that, by God's grace or by
men's good will, there'll be peace for him and all go well,
she finds some fault with him and starts a fight. For where
there is a woman in the house, no one can ask
a friend to come and stay with him, and still feel safe.
Even the wife who appears to be the best-behaved
turns out to be the one who lets herself go wrong.
Her husband gawps and doesn't notice; neighbors do,
and smile to see how still another man gets fooled.
Each man will pick the faults in someone else's wife
and boast of his own each time he speaks of her. And yet
the same thing happens to us all. But we don't see.
For women are the biggest single bad thing Zeus
has made for us; a ball-and-chain; we can't get loose
since that time when the fight about a wife began
the Great War, and they volunteered, and went to hell.

2 · *The Vanity of Human Wishes*

My child, Zeus the deep-thundering holds the ends of all
actions in his own hands, disposes as he will
of everything. We who are human have no minds,
but live, from day to day, like beasts and nothing know
of what God plans to make happen to each of us.
But hope and self-persuasion keep us all alive
in our unprofitable desires. Some watch the day
for what it brings, and some the turn of years, and none
so downcast he will not believe that time to come
will make him virtuous, rich, all his heart's desire.
But other things begin to happen first; old age,
which no one wants, gets one before he makes his goal.
Painful diseases wear down some; others are killed

in battle, and death takes them under the dark earth.
Some, battered in the sudden hurricane on the sea,
where waves crowd big across the blue salt water, drown
and die, when all they looked for was some way to live.
Some loop (a dismal way to die) the noose around
their necks and go self-murdered from the sunlight. Thus
no evil thing is missing. In their thousands stand
bad spirits, and innumerable griefs, and pains
about our life. If men would take advice from me,
we should not long for what is really bad, nor buy
our heart's own torment for our hard work done in vain.

· 3 ·

The time of afterdeath for us is very long.
We live a wretched sum of years, and badly, too.

· 4 ·

No better thing befalls a man than a good wife,
no worse thing than a bad one.

· 5 ·

A woman thick around the ankles is no good.

HIPPÓNAX
OF ÉPHESOS

The evidence for the date of Hippónax is conflicting, but his chief time of
activity would seem to fall in the first half of the sixth century, for it is strik-
ing that he never mentions the great Persian invasion, which began shortly
after 550. Hippónax invented the *choliambic*, sometimes called *scazon*, or "lame
iambic," reversing the stress at the end of the line so as to bring the reader
(listener) down on the wrong foot. His own name placed at the end of a
line (3) gives this effect and may well have suggested the meter. He also

wrote "lame trochaics"; the fourth is an example. The fragments are numerous, but very short, and present no continuity; what there is shows bold use of colloquialisms, a caustic humor, and the ear of a master.

· 1 ·

Hermes, dear Hermes, Maia's son from Kylléne,
I pray to you, I'm suffering from extreme shivers,
so give an overcoat to Hippónax, give him
a cape, and sandals, and felt overshoes, sixty
pieces of gold to bury in his strong chamber.

· 2 ·

Keep traveling, you swine, the whole way toward Smyrna.
Go through the Lydian land, past the tomb of Alyáttes,
the grave of Gyges and the pillar of Megástrys,
the monument of Atys, son of Alyáttes,
big chief, and point your paunch against the sun's setting.

· 3 ·

The God of Wealth, who's altogether blind, never
came walking in my door and told me: "Hippónax,
I'm giving you three hundred silver mna pieces,
and much beside." Not he. He's far too mean-hearted.

· 4 ·

Hold my jacket, somebody, while I hit Boúpalos in the eye.
I can hit with both hands, and I never miss punches.

TYRTAÉUS
OF SPARTA

Tyrtaéus was active at Sparta during the Second Messenian War, that is, in the second half of the seventh century. He is said to have been a foreigner invited in from Athens or Míletus, but he may have been a Spartan born. Later

writers also make him a general and a statesman, but he probably was simply
a poet writing in a semi-official capacity. I, at least, cannot imagine a general,
even in the seventh century, instructing his troops to set their teeth and shake
terribly the crests of their helmets. His over-all duty may rather have been to
inspire the Spartiates with love for order, obedience to the laws, and military
valor.

1 · *Courage: heros mortuus: heros vivus*

I would not say anything for a man nor take account of him
    for any speed of his feet or wrestling skill he might have,
not if he had the size of a Cyclops and strength to go with it,
    not if he could outrun Bóreas, the North Wind of Thrace,
not if he were more handsome and gracefully formed than Tithónos,
    or had more riches than Midas had, or Kínyras too,
not if he were more of a king than Tantalid Pelops,
    or had the power of speech and persuasion Adrastos had,
not if he had all splendors except for a fighting spirit.
    For no man ever proves himself a good man in war
unless he can endure to face the blood and the slaughter,
    go close against the enemy and fight with his hands.
Here is courage, mankind's finest possession, here is
    the noblest prize that a young man can endeavor to win,
and it is a good thing his city and all the people share with him
    when a man plants his feet and stands in the foremost spears
relentlessly, all thought of foul flight completely forgotten,
    and has well trained his heart to be steadfast and to endure,
and with words encourages the man who is stationed beside him.
    Here is a man who proves himself to be valiant in war.
With a sudden rush he turns to flight the rugged battalions
    of the enemy, and sustains the beating waves of assault.
And he who so falls among the champions and loses his sweet life,
    so blessing with honor his city, his father, and all his people,
with wounds in his chest, where the spear that he was facing has
    transfixed
    that massive guard of his shield, and gone through his breastplate
      as well,
why, such a man is lamented alike by the young and the elders,
    and all his city goes into mourning and grieves for his loss.

His tomb is pointed to with pride, and so are his children,
    and his children's children, and afterward all the race that is his.
His shining glory is never forgotten, his name is remembered,
    and he becomes an immortal, though he lies under the ground,
when one who was a brave man has been killed by the furious War God
    standing his ground and fighting hard for his children and land.
But if he escapes the doom of death, the destroyer of bodies,
    and wins his battle, and bright renown for the work of his spear,
all men give place to him alike, the youth and the elders,
    and much joy comes his way before he goes down to the dead.
Aging, he has reputation among his citizens. No one
    tries to interfere with his honors or all he deserves;
all men withdraw before his presence, and yield their seats to him,
    the youth, and the men his age, and even those older than he.
Thus a man should endeavor to reach this high place of courage
    with all his heart, and, so trying, never be backward in war.

2 · *To the Soldiers, after a Defeat*

Now, since you are the seed of Herakles the invincible,
    courage! Zeus has not yet turned away from us. Do not
fear the multitude of their men, nor run away from them.
    Each man should bear his shield straight at the foremost ranks
and make his heart a thing full of hate, and hold the black flying
    spirits of death as dear as he holds the flash of the sun.
You know what havoc is the work of the painful War God,
    you have learned well how things go in exhausting war,
for you have been with those who ran and with the pursuers,
    O young men, you have had as much of both as you want.
Those who, standing their ground and closing their ranks together,
    endure the onset at close quarters and fight in the front,
they lose fewer men. They also protect the army behind them.
    Once they flinch, the spirit of the whole army falls apart.
And no man could count over and tell all the number of evils,
    all that can come to a man, once he gives way to disgrace.
For once a man reverses and runs in the terror of battle,
    he offers his back, a tempting mark to spear from behind,
and it is a shameful sight when a dead man lies in the dust there,
    driven through from behind by the stroke of an enemy spear.

No, no, let him take a wide stance and stand up strongly against them,
   digging both heels in the ground, biting his lip with his teeth,
covering thighs and legs beneath, his chest and his shoulders
   under the hollowed-out protection of his broad shield,
while in his right hand he brandishes the powerful war-spear,
   and shakes terribly the crest high above his helm.
Our man should be disciplined in the work of the heavy fighter,
   and not stand out from the missiles when he carries a shield,
but go right up and fight at close quarters and, with his long spear
   or short sword, thrust home and strike his enemy down.
Let him fight toe to toe and shield against shield hard driven,
   crest against crest and helmet on helmet, chest against chest;
let him close hard and fight it out with his opposite foeman,
   holding tight to the hilt of his sword, or to his long spear.
And you, O light-armed fighters, from shield to shield of your fellows
   dodge for protection and keep steadily throwing great stones,
and keep on pelting the enemy with your javelins, only
   remember always to stand near your own heavy-armed men.

MIMNÉRMUS
OF CÓLOPHON

Mimnérmus seems to have lived from the middle of the seventh to the be-
ginning of the sixth century and to have written numerous short pieces and a
long poem (or connected series) in elegiac meter which contained historical
material.

· 1 ·

What, then, is life if love the golden is gone? What is pleasure?
   Better to die when the thought of these is lost from my heart:
the flattery of surrender, the secret embrace in the darkness.
   These alone are such charming flowers of youth as befall
women and men. But once old age with its sorrows advances
   upon us, it makes a man feeble and ugly alike,
heart worn thin with the hovering expectation of evil,

lost all joy that comes out of the sight of the sun.
Hateful to boys a man goes then, unfavored of women.
   Such is the thing of sorrow God has made of old age.

· 2 ·

All his days Hélios, the Sun, has hard work for his portion.
   Never is there any pause for rest that is given to him,
either himself or his horses, once Dawn of the rosy fingers,
   leaving the Ocean waters goes on her way, up the sky.
For Hélios is carried across the sea-waves in a wondrous
   hollow cup for a bed, the work of Hephaístos' hands,
made of precious gold, and with wings. Over the sea's surface
   it carries him, gratefully sleeping, from the Hespérides' shore
to the Ethiopians' country. There he keeps his swift chariot and
      horses
   waiting, until the Dawn, the early child, shall arrive.

3 · *The Warrior of the Past*

None could match the strength of him and the pride of his courage.
   Thus the tale told of my fathers who saw him there
breaking the massed battalions of armored Lydian horsemen,
   swinging the ashwood spear on the range of the Hermos plain.
Pallas Athene, goddess of war, would have found no fault with
   this stark heart in its strength, when at the first-line rush
swift in the blood and staggered collision of armies in battle
   all through the raining shafts he fought out a bitter path.
No man ever in the strong encounters of battle was braver
   than he, when he went still in the gleaming light of the sun.

All Solon's poetry refers to autocracy, oppressive aristocracy, tyrants & tyranny, money & poverty, social unrest, civil strife etc

SOLON
OF ATHENS

Solon was the great social reformer, whose long life seems to have extended from about 630 to 550 or later. In either 594 or 592 he was made archon with extraordinary powers. He abolished all debts in which the person of the debtor was mortgaged and set free all who had been enslaved for debt, but he refused to redistribute property. His aim was to mitigate social injustice by moderate compromise before the underprivileged should become so exasperated that they would look for a dictator ("tyrant") to lead them. Many expected, and hoped in fact, that Solon would make himself dictator, but he refused to do this.

Solon also reformed the constitution. His fame rests mainly on his social and political work, but he was also a soldier, a merchant and traveler, a reflective thinker, the first identifiable "man of letters" in Athens, and a poet of considerable imagination and eloquence. Some of his poems (such as 2, 3, and 4) were composed in defense of his policies. Others are purely contemplative.

1 · *Prayer to the Muses*

Shining daughters of Memory and Zeus on Olympus,
    Muses, Piérides, listen to me in my prayers.
Grant me, at the hands of the blessed immortals, prosperity,
    and always a high degree in the opinion of men.
So shall I bring pleasure to friends and pain to my enemies,
    and my friends look on me in admiration, the others in fear.

Wealth My desire is to have riches; but win them unjustly
    I will not, for retribution must then come my way.
When it is gods who are giving it, wealth befalls a man as some
    solid plant, firm set from base of stock to the crest;
but cultivated with violence, it comes against nature, *against violence*
    dragged and obedient under direction of crimes,
all unwilling it follows, and ruin is there in a moment.
    The beginning of disaster is not much, as when a fire
burns small in its first stages and ends in catastrophe. As fire's
    course is, such is the course taken by human misdeeds.
But Zeus forever is watching the end, and strikes of a sudden,

« 18 »

as when a storm in spring abruptly scatters the clouds
and dredges up from the depth the open and heaving water
   where waves roll, and sweeping on across the generous land,
leaves in wreckage fair work men have done, till it hits the headlong
   sky, the gods' home, and the air is shining on every side
you look, and the blaze of the sun breaks out on the fertile acres
   in all its splendor, and there are no more clouds to be seen.
Such is the punishment Zeus gives, he does not, like a mortal,
   fall in a rage over each particular thing, and yet
it never escapes him all the way when a man has a sinful
   spirit; and always, in the end, his judgment is plain.
One man has to pay at once, one later, while others
   altogether escape overtaking by the gods' doom;
but then it always comes in aftertime, and the innocent
   pay, the sons of the sinners or those born long afterward.

But here is how we men, be we good, be we evil,
   think. Each keeps his own personal notion within
until he suffers. Then he cries out, but all until such time
   we take our idiot beguilement in light-weight hopes,
and one who is stricken and worn out in lingering sickness
   has taken measures and thinks he will grow healthy, and one *coward*
who is a coward expects to turn into a warlike hero.
   Another, ugly, thinks of the day when his looks will charm.
If one be penniless and sunk in the struggle of poverty,
   he, too, dreams upon the possession of huge estates.
They all rush off on their various business. One goes seafaring
   across the wide sea, in ships, where the fish swarm, trying to bring
a little money home, at the mercy of brutal hurricanes,
   no hard bargainer for his own life. While another, one
of those whose living is won by the bent plowshare and hard labor,
   furrows, year in year out, the tilth of his orchard ground.
One, who has learned Hepháistos' arts and the arts of Athene
   and all their skills, by work of his hands assembles a wage.
Yet another, dowered by the grace of Olympian Muses,
   has learned control of loveliness in the wisdom of verse.
One the lord far-ranging, Apollo, has made a soothsayer.
   He sees the evil coming from far away to a man
when the gods grant such knowledge; yet there is no way for bird sign

nor sacrifice to ward off that which is fated to be.
Others, who understand the works of Paion with all his
   drugs, are healers. But neither are these complete in their craft,
seeing that often from a small pain grows a big affliction
   and no one, by giving mild remedies, can take it away,
while another, who is in agony from wasting afflictions,
   can suddenly be healed by a simple touch of the hand.
Fate brings humanity her good; she brings him her evil;
   and what the gods give us for gifts no man can refuse.
Danger, for all, lies in all action, and there is no telling
   which way the end will be after a thing is begun.
One may be trying to do well and, through failure of foresight,
   may fall into the curse of great disaster, while one
who acts badly may find God gives him all that he asked for,
   sheer good luck, that sets him free from the fault of his mind.
But money; there is no end of its making in human endeavor.
   Those among us who have already the biggest estates
try to get twice as much as they have. Who can satisfy all of them?
   Money, when a man makes it, is the gift of the gods,
but disaster can grow out of money, and when retribution
   comes at the sending of Zeus, none can tell where it will light.

2 · Political Verses

This city of ours will never be destroyed by the planning
   of Zeus, nor according to the wish of the immortal gods;
such is she who, great hearted, mightily fathered, protects us,
   Pallas Athene, whose hands are stretched out over our heads.
But the citizens themselves in their wildness are bent on destruction
   of their great city, and money is the compulsive cause.
The leaders of the people are evil-minded. The next stage
   will be great suffering, recompense for their violent acts,
for they do not know enough to restrain their greed and apportion
   orderly shares for all as if at a decorous feast.

. . . .
   they are tempted into unrighteous acts and grow rich.
. . . .

   sparing the property neither of the public nor of the gods,
they go on stealing, by force or deception, each from the other,

nor do the solemn commitments of Justice keep them in check;
but she knows well, though silent, what happens and what has been
    happening,
  and in her time she returns to extract a full revenge;
for it comes upon the entire city as a wound beyond healing,
  and quickly it happens that foul slavery is the result,
and slavery wakens internal strife, and sleeping warfare,
  and this again destroys many in the pride of their youth,
for from enemies' devising our much-adored city is afflicted
  before long by conspiracies so dear to wicked men.
Such evils are churning in the home country, but, of the impoverished,
  many have made their way abroad on to alien soil,
sold away, and shamefully going in chains of slavery . . .

. . . .

Thus the public Ruin invades the house of each citizen,
  and the courtyard doors no longer have strength to keep it away,
but it overleaps the lofty wall, and though a man runs in
  and tries to hide in chamber or closet, it ferrets him out.
So my spirit dictates to me: I must tell the Athenians
  how many evils a city suffers from Bad Government,
and how Good Government displays all neatness and order, *lawbreakers*
  and many times she must put shackles on the breakers of laws.
She levels rough places, stops Glut and Greed, takes the force from
    Violence;
  she dries up the growing flowers of Despair as they grow;
she straightens out crooked judgments given, gentles the swollen
  ambitions, and puts an end to acts of divisional strife;
she stills the gall of wearisome Hate, and under her influence
  all life among mankind is harmonious and does well.

· 3 ·

I gave the people as much privilege as they have a right to:
  I neither degraded them from rank nor gave them free hand;
and for those who already held the power and were envied for money,
  I worked it out that they also should have no cause for complaint.
I stood there holding my sturdy shield over both the parties;
  I would not let either side win a victory that was wrong.

In defense of his political policies

. . . .

Thus would the people be best off, with the leaders they follow:
  neither given excessive freedom nor put to restraint;
for Glut gives birth to Greed, when great prosperity suddenly
  befalls those people who do not have an orderly mind.

. . . .

Acting where issues are great, it is hard to please all.

4 · *In Defense of His Policies*

My purpose was to bring my scattered people back
together. Where did I fall short of my design?
I call to witness at the judgment seat of time
one who is noblest, mother of Olympian
divinities, and greatest of them all, Black Earth.
I took away the mortgage stones stuck in her breast,
and she, who went a slave before, is now set free.
Into this sacred land, our Athens, I brought back
a throng of those who had been sold, some by due law,
though others wrongly; some by hardship pressed to escape
the debts they owed; and some of these no longer spoke
Attic, since they had drifted wide around the world,
while those in the country had the shame of slavery
upon them, and they served their masters' moods in fear.
These I set free; and I did this by strength of hand,
welding right law with violence to a single whole.
So have I done, and carried through all that I pledged.
I have made laws, for the good man and the bad alike,
and shaped a rule to suit each case, and set it down.
Had someone else not like myself taken the reins,
some ill-advised or greedy person, he would not
have held the people in. Had I agreed to do
what pleased their adversaries at that time, or what
they themselves planned to do against their enemies,
our city would have been widowed of her men. Therefore,
I put myself on guard at every side, and turned
among them like a wolf inside a pack of dogs.

« 22 »

5 · *The Ten Ages of Man* *7 year periods*

A child in his infancy grows his first set of teeth and loses them *1-7*
   within seven years. For so long he counts as only a child.
When God has brought to accomplishment the next seven-year period, *7-14*
   one shows upon his body the signs of maturing youth.
In the third period he is still getting his growth, while on his chin *14-21*
   the beard comes, to show he is turning from youth to a man.
The fourth seven years are the time when every man reaches his *21-28*
      highest
   point of physical strength where men look for prowess achieved.
In the fifth period the time is ripe for a young man *28-35*
   to think of marriage and children, a family to be raised.
The mind of a man comes to full maturity in the sixth period, *35-42*
   but he cannot now do as much, nor does he wish that he could.
In the seventh period of seven years and in the eighth also *42-49*
   for fourteen years in all, his speech is best in his life. *49-56*
He can still do much in his ninth period, but there is a weakening *56-63*
   seen in his ability both to think and to speak.
But if he completes ten ages of seven years each, full measure, *63-70*
   death, when it comes, can no longer be said to come too soon.

PHOCÝLIDES

OF MÍLETUS

Phocýlides is placed in the middle of the sixth century. His specialty was
gnomai, epigrams brief and pointed, and frequently beginning with his "sig-
nature," as shown in the specimens here translated.

· 1 ·

Phocýlides said this also: a city that's small and is founded
on a cliff's edge, well governed, is stronger than Nineveh crazy.

· 2 ·

Phocýlides said this also: Lérians are bad: not one bad, one not:
all bad: except Prokles: and Prokles is Lérian too.

· 3 ·

Phocýlides said this also: What good does it do to be well born
for those whose words bring pleasure to none, nor their characters
either?

Aristocracy

XENÓPHANES
OF CÓLOPHON

On the basis of the third poem, Xenóphanes can be estimated to have lived
from about 570 to some time after 480 B.C., since the career he speaks of prob-
ably began when he left Cólophon to escape the Persians in about 545 and
migrated to Élea on the Italian coast south of Naples. There he founded the
philosophical school called Eleátic, his successors being Parménides and Zeno.
All were monists. Xenóphanes is generally thought of more as a philosopher
than as a poet, but he wrote verse extensively. Poems 1 and 2 both anticipate
Socrates and Plato. It was Socrates who proposed that, as a "fair recompense
for his activities," he should be maintained at the public expense in the Athe-
nian capitol (in preference to victorious athletes, Plato, *Apol.* 36d). In the
Symposium of Plato, it is urged that the guests at the symposium (drinking
party) dismiss the flute girl (floor show?) and turn their energies to serious
discussion (*Symposium* 176e).

1 · *The Well-Tempered Symposium*

Now the floor is swept clean, and the hands of all who are present
    are washed, and the cups are clean. One puts the garlands on,
another passes the fragrant myrrh on a dish. The mixing
    bowl is set up and stands by, full of the spirit of cheer,
and more wine still stands ready and promises no disappointment;
    sweet wine, in earthen jars, preserving its own bouquet.
In the middle of all, frankincense gives out its holy fragrance,
    and we have water there too, cold and crystal and sweet.

Golden-brown loaves are set nearby, and the lordly table
　　is weighted down underneath its load of honey and cheese.
The altar, in the center, is completely hidden in flowers.
　　Merriment and singing fill all the corners of the house.
First of all, enlightened men should hymn the God, using
　　words of propriety, and stories that have no fault.
Then, when they have made libation and prayed to be able
　　to conduct themselves like gentlemen as occasion demands,
it will not be drunk-and-disorderly to drink as much as one can
　　and still get home without help—except for a very old man.
Best approve that man who in drinking discloses notable
　　ideas, as they come to his mind and his good disposition directs.
It's no use to tell the tale of the battles of Titans and Giants,
　　or Centaurs either, those fictions of our fathers' imaginations,
nor wars of the Gods; there's no good to be got from such subjects.
　　One should be thoughtful always and right-minded toward the
　　Gods.

2 · *The Athlete and the Philosopher*

Now, supposing a man were to win the prize for the foot race
　　at Olýmpia, there where the precinct of Zeus stands beside
the river, at Pisa: or if he wins the five-contests, or the wrestling,
　　or if he endures the pain of boxing and wins, or that new
and terrible game they call the pankrátion, contest of all holds:
　　why, such a man will obtain honor, in the citizens' sight,
and be given a front seat and be on display at all civic occasions,
　　and he would be given his meals all at the public expense,
and be given a gift from the city to take and store for safekeeping.
　　If he won with the chariot, too, all this would be granted to him,
and yet he would not deserve it, as I do. Better than brute strength
　　of men, or horses either, is the wisdom that is mine.
But custom is careless in all these matters, and there is no justice
　　in putting strength on a level above wisdom which is sound.
For if among the people there is one who is a good boxer,
　　or one who excels in wrestling or in the five-contests,
or else for speed of his feet, and this is prized beyond other
　　feats of strength that men display in athletic games,
the city will not, on account of this man, have better government.

Small is the pleasure the city derives from one of its men
    if he happens to come first in the games by the banks of Pisa.
This does not make rich the treasure house of the state.

3 · On His Career and Age

Now the Years are seven and sixty that have been tossing
    my restless intelligence up and down the land of the Greeks,
and to these there are five and twenty more still to be added
    before I began: at least if my addition is right.

THEÓGNIS
OF MÉGARA

Alone among the poets here represented (except Pindar), Theógnis sur-
vives not through fragments but in a manuscript of his own. This, however,
has produced its own puzzle. What we have is a long series of elegies, of
varying individual lengths, running to nearly 1,400 lines. This contains, with
slight variations, poems elsewhere ascribed to Tyrtaéus, Mimnérmus, and
Solon, and it seems likely that the work of Theógnis himself may have formed
the basis for some sort of anthology. Lines 19–26 obviously bear on this prob-
lem, but do nothing to solve it. The poems addressed to Kyrnos, son of Póly-
pas, are the ones most likely to belong to Theógnis himself. The Simónides
addressed in 667 may or may not be the famous poet from Ceos.

Theógnis himself came from Mégara and lived in the middle or later sixth
century and probably into the fifth. The poems in this collection had a dem-
onstrably strong influence on Athenian writers, particularly Euripides and
Plato.

· 19–26 ·

Kyrnos, this is my work; let a seal be stamped on the writing
    of these words, so that none who steals them shall ever deceive,
so that none in the presence of good work can substitute forgery.
    Thus shall each reader say: "These are the words of Theógnis
of Mégara, a great name, the world knows it." And yet
    I cannot please all the people in my own town.
No wonder there, son of Pólypas, since not Zeus even
    can please all, by raining or withholding his rain.

· 39–52 ·

Kyrnos, this city is big with child, and I fear it will bring forth
  a man who will chastise all our disorderly ways.
The people in the city are still well behaved, but their leaders *aristocracy*
  have turned their steps into a path that will make them corrupt.
Never yet, my Kyrnos, was a city destroyed by its nobles,
  but only after base men take to disorderly ways,
and debauch their own people and give rights to the unrighteous
  for the sake of their own money and power; and when this is so,
hold no hope for such a city to remain unshaken
  for long, although for the time it rides on a tranquil keel,
not when such activities have tempted the base men
  and private advantage comes with public disaster. For this
breeds civil discord and men's blood shed by their fellow-citizens,
  and monarchies. But pray that our city may never be such.

· 53–68 ·

Kyrnos, this city is still the same city, but its people are different.
  Those who before knew nothing of lawsuits, nothing of laws,
who went about in goatskins flapping over their shoulders,
  who lived on the ranges, far out from the town, like wild deer,
these are now the Great Men, son of Pólypas. Our former nobles *aristocracy*
  are Rabble now. Who could endure it when things are so?
They swindle each other, they mock at one another, and meanwhile
  understand nothing at all of what good and bad men think.
Never make one of these citizens your friend, son of Pólypas,
  however much you may need to use them: not from the heart:
pretend to all that you are their friend: talk as if you were one:
  but never communicate to any one of these men
anything important. You must know that their purposes are unpleasant,
  and there is no trusting them in any matter at all,
but treachery, and deception, and catch-as-catch-can is their nature.
  Such are the desperate men who have no future assured.

· 119–24 ·

Spurious gold and silver are an endurable evil,
  Kyrnos, and give no difficulty to the skilled man

to know what they are. But if the mind in a friend is secretly
    false and he carries a heart of trickery hidden within,
this, of all God's works among men, is the thing most spurious
    and most evil, since such deception can never be seen.

· 133–42 ·

No man, Kyrnos, is responsible for his own disasters
    or gains, but both alike are handed out by the gods;
nor does any human being who acts have any true knowledge
    whether the thing he does will end in evil or good.
Often he thinks the result will be bad, and it comes out better;
    he thinks again the result will be good, and it comes out worse.
Nor is what happens to any person just what he wishes.
    We are helpless: it is hard: but we are caught and confined.
We are men, what we think is vanity, for we know nothing.
    All is disposed of by the gods in the way they wish.

· 151–52 ·

Kyrnos, when God intends to make a city desolate,
    he inspires violence in one of its evil men.

· 183–86 ·

Kyrnos, when we are breeding stock, we look for the best in
    horses, donkeys, or rams for stud, to get a good strain;
yet even the finest man is willing to marry a rascal's
    rascally daughter, if only she brings him money enough.

· 213–18 ·

Kyrnos, be flexible in character, always adapting
    your own mood to that of the friend you chance to be with;
be as the lithe and tentacled octopus, altering color
    so that it matches and loses itself in the rock where it clings;
so be you; be now like this, then change your complexion;
    better you should be subtle than stubbornly always the same.

· 237–54 ·

See, I have given you wings on which to hover uplifted
   high above earth entire and the great waste of the sea
without strain. Wherever men meet in festivals, as men
   gather, you will be there, your name will be spoken again
as the young singers, with the flutes clear piping beside them,
   make you into a part of the winsome verses, and sing
of you. And even after you pass to the gloom and the secret
   chambers of sorrow, Death's house hidden under the ground,
even in death your memory shall not pass, and it shall not
   die, but always, a name and a song in the minds of men,
Kyrnos, you shall outrange the land of Greece and the islands,
   cross the upheaving sea where the fish swarm, carried not
astride the back of a horse, but the shining gifts of the dark-wreathed
   Muses shall be the force that carries you on your way.
For all wherever song is you shall be there for the singers.
   So long as earth endures and sun endures, you shall be.
I did this. But you give me not the smallest attention.
   You put me off with deceits as if I were a little child.

· 325–26 ·

Try for nothing excessive. The middle degree is best. So,
   Kyrnos, you will win virtue, a difficult thing to attain.

· 577–78 ·

It is easier to make bad out of good than good out of evil.
   Never try to teach me. I am too old to be taught.

· 667–82 ·

If I had money, Simónides, as I have had in time past,
   I could without embarrassment consort with the great.
But as it is, I know a man, and he passes me by. Dumb
   stand I, for poverty, though I know as much as the rest
even now. So it is. We are swept with the wind, white sails lost,
   out from the Melian Sea, on into the gloom of the night.

The men are unwilling to bail any more. The sea washes over
  the bulwarks on either side, and barely and in distress
we keep afloat. But some are at work. They have put down the noble
  helmsman, who knew his business well, and kept a good watch.
All discipline is gone, and they plunder the cargo at random,
  nor is there any fair division made for the lot.
The base hands and the porters control, the great are beneath them.
  I am afraid. I think the sea will swallow our ship.
Let this be my secret cipher addressed to the nobles;
  but even the base man, if he is clever, can see what it means.

· 699–718 ·

For the multitude of mankind there is only one virtue:
  Money. And there was no good found in anything else,
not if you had the sagacity of the great Rhadamánthys,
  not if you had the resource of Sísyphos, Aíolos' son,
who by the crafty guile in his mind came up out of Hades
  and flattered the Queen of the Dead into letting him go,
Persephone, who dims men's mind with the water of Lethe;
  and to this day no other man has made such an escape,
once the darkness of death has closed in a vapor about him,
  once he has taken his way to the shadowy place of the dead
and gone on through the black gates which shut the protesting
  souls of dead men in and will not let them go free;
yet Sísyphos was a hero who came back even from that place
  into the light of the sun through the resource in his mind;
not if you could be false and make falsehood look like honesty,
  not if you had fair speech like Nestor the almost-divine,
not if in the speed of your feet you outran the flying
  Harpies or the North Wind's two sons in the storm of their feet.
None of these; but all men must understand when I tell them:
  Money, and nothing but Money, holds all the power in the world.

· 783–88 ·

I have been in my time as far as the land of Sicily.
  I have been to Euboía, where vineyards grow in the plain,
and Sparta, the shining city by the reedy banks of Eurótas;

and everywhere I was met with enthusiasm and love,
but my heart has taken no joy from the attentions of strangers.
A man's own country is dearest. This is the truth in the end.

· 869–72 ·

May wide and towering heaven collapse upon me in all its
bronze and terror, catastrophe to the peoples of earth,
on that day when I no longer stand by my companions,
on that day when I cease to harry my enemies.

· 1197–1202 ·

I heard the voice of that bird, son of Pólypas, whose piercing outcry
and whose arrival announces to men the season when fields
are plowed, and the voice of her broke the heart that darkens with-
in me,
since other men possess my flourishing acres now,
and not for me are the mules dragging the plow through the grainland,
since I have given my heart to the restless seafarer's life.

EARLY METRICAL INSCRIPTIONS

The practice of inscribing verses on stone began in the seventh century.
Most Greek metrical inscriptions are sepulchral; some are attached to votive
offerings. Late Greek and Roman metrical inscriptions sometimes run to great
length and ornate style, but I have confined myself to a few examples of the
severe early manner. Among these, however, the epitaph for Téttichos (which
was partly copied in an epitaph from Argos), with its appeal to the wayfarer,
gives some indication of the style to come.

Simónides of Ceos wrote inscribed epigrams, though he has undoubtedly
been saddled with some that were not from his hand. Anácreon and Archílo-
chus probably wrote them, and Sappho may have done so. Those included
here were probably done by amateurs; and the poet does not sign, except for
the third, where the name may be that of the poet, or the stonecutter, or the
two may have been identical.

The inscriptions are from stones, except the seventh, which was written on
gold leaf and found in a tomb.

1 · Corinth

This is the tomb of Deínias killed by the cruel sea.

2 · Piraeus (Attica)

The memorial to the skill of Aineías, best of physicians.

3 · Athens

Achérmos of Chios made me.
Iphídike dedicated me to Athene Keeper of Cities.

4 · Thasos

When Leárete died her father set up a monument
which has beauty. But we shall nevermore see her alive.

5 · Attica

The tomb of Phrasikleía: I shall be called maiden forever.
This, not wife, is the title the gods gave me for mine.

6 · Attica

Whether you are a citizen or a stranger coming from elsewhere,
take pity on Téttichos as you pass by: a brave man
killed in battle, who there lost the pride of his fresh youth.
Mourn for him a while, and go on. May your fortune be good.

7 · Petelia, Italy

You will find to the left of the house of Hades a wellspring,
and by the side of this standing a white cypress.
You must not even go close to this wellspring; but also
you will find another spring that comes from the lake of Memory
cold water running, and there are those who stand guard before it.
You shall say: "I am a child of earth and the starry heavens,
but my generation is of the sky. You yourselves know this.
But I am dry with thirst and am dying. Give me then quickly
the water that runs cold out of the lake of Memory."
And they themselves will give you to drink from the sacred water,
and afterward you shall be lord among the rest of the heroes.

TERPÁNDER
OF ANTÍSSA (LESBOS)

Terpánder appears to have been active in the middle of the seventh century, and thus was roughly contemporary with Archílochus and Callínus, perhaps actually a little older than they. He was clearly a figure of very great importance in the history of Greek music and choral lyric, and had much to do with making Sparta, which seems to have been his second home, a center of choral poetry. Very little, however, is left of his work.

Sparta

There flowers the battle-spear of young men, there the Muse is eloquent,
there Justice in the wide ways lends force to actions of honor.

ALCMAN
OF SPARTA

Alcman is sometimes thought to have been a Lydian from Sardis. The idea comes from the fifth poem, although nothing proves that he is talking about himself. He was probably a Spartan, possibly a Messénian. Definitely younger than Terpánder, he was active in the later seventh century. The only large fragment is the Maiden Song (1), which is here represented only by the second half; the first, which deals with an exploit of Kastor and Polydeúkes, is too badly preserved to translate, and the part given here, though charming, is full of insoluble puzzles. It is clear, however, that Alcman anticipated Stesíchorus and Pindar, both in the matter of triads (strophe, antistrophe, epode) and in the Pindaric habit of combining heroic legend with contemporary occasions and persons (we cannot tell whether or not Stesíchorus did this).

1 · Maiden Song

There is vengeance from the gods;
but blessed is he who blithely

winds out all his day of life
without tears. But I must sing the
light of Ágido. I see
her like the sun, whose shining
on us is witnessed through Ágido.
But our lovely choir leader
will not let me praise her, nor
say she is not fair.
She knows well that she herself is
something dazzling,
just as if among a herd of
cattle one should set a racehorse,
sinewy, swift, and with feet full of thunder,
creature out of a dream with wings.

Look and see. That other is
like a fleet Venetian courser,
but the tresses of my cousin
Hagesíchora! They blossom
into gold without alloy,
and her face is pale like silver.
Must I tell you this so plainly?
There is Hagesíchora.
Loveliest after Ágido,
she will still run,
Lydian horse with Scythian racer
close together;
for the Pleiades against us,
as we carry Órthria's plow
through the divine night, rise up to strive
        with us,
blazing bright as a single star.

Luxury of purple dye,
all we have can never help us,
not the carven bracelet-snake,
not the wimple sheer in gold
Lydian, the pride and glory
of the girls with delicate eyes,

not the hair of Nanno, not
Áreta's immortal beauty,
never Kleasísera,
not Thúlakis,
nor go to Ainesímbrota's
house and say:
Let Ástaphis be on my side;
let Philýlla look my way;
give me Damáreta, lovely Iánthemis.
Hagesíchora is all our hope.

Is not Hagesíchora
of the lovely step here beside us?
Does she wait with Ágido,
and with her commend our performance?
But you Gods, accept their prayers,
for the end and the achievement
come from God. My chorus leader,
maiden as I am, I say
I have only shrilled in vain
from the roof tops
like an owl; yet I would also
please our Lady
of the Dawn; for it was she who
came to heal us of our trouble.
Maidens, we have come to the peace desired,
all through Hagesíchora's grace.

All the chariot's course is swung
to the running of the trace-horse,
all the ship must come to heel,
swiftly to the captain's handling.
She has sung her song today
not more sweetly than the sirens
(they are gods). But how we sang,
we ten girls instead of the Eleven!
One is trilling like a swan by
Xanthos river,
one with splendid tawny hair. . . .

· 2 ·

This is not Aphrodite, but the lewd Love-boy, playing
like a child, running the flowers, across the do-not-touch-me meadow
    grass.

· 3 ·

No longer, maiden voices sweet-calling, sounds of allurement,
can my limbs bear me up; oh I wish, I wish I could be a seabird
who with halcyons skims the surf-flowers of the sea water
with careless heart, a sea-blue-colored and sacred waterfowl.

· 4 ·

Counterbalanced against the iron is the sweet lyre-playing.

· 5 ·

You are no country fellow, neither
lout nor pigkeeper:
not Thessálian born: neither
Erysichaían: not a sheepman:
but come from high Sardis.

STESÍCHORUS
OF HÍMERA

The name Stesíchorus, "arranger of chorales," suggests a family in which
choral poetry was a traditional occupation. There were, apparently, several
poets so named. An early but quite unreliable series of notices would make the
first Stesíchorus the son of Hesiod. There is, however, good evidence for a
Stesíchorus who lived from the later seventh to the middle sixth century. He
was born, probably, at Mataúros in southern Italy, but made his home at
Hímera in Sicily. He wrote long choral lyrics in complex structures and in
them told stories from the heroic cycles. He probably had a very considerable
influence not only on Pindar but also on Aeschylus (he wrote an *Oresteía*),
and he is the first great name in West-Greek poetry. But Stesíchorus has

shared the fate of Terpánder. His importance is unquestioned, but his work survives only in very short fragments which give little idea of what he could really do. We have a much better impression of the less influential Alcman through possession of one good-sized piece.

Stesíchorus is said to have lost his sight for slandering Helen. He apologized, by perpetuating the story that she never went to Troy at all, and regained his sight.

1 · *Helen and Klytaimestra*

So once, when Tyndareus
made sacrifices to all the gods, he forgot one only, the giver of blessings,
Aphrodite. And she in anger
with the daughters of Tyndareus made them twice married and three
    times married
and brides who deserted their husbands.

2 · *Palinode to Helen*

That story is not true.
You never sailed in the benched ships.
You never went to the city of Troy.

ÍBYCUS
OF RHÉGIUM

Íbycus was active in the second half of the sixth century. Like Stesíchorus a Western Greek, he traveled widely and appears to have made a good living out of choral poetry. He also, I think, wrote lyric monody, of which the selection in the text is probably an example.

In spring time the Kydonian
quinces, watered by running streams,
there where the maiden nymphs have
their secret garden, and grapes that grow
round in shade of the tendriled vine,
ripen.

Now in this season for me
there is no rest from love.
Out of the hard bright sky,
a Thracian north wind blowing
with searing rages and hurt—dark,
pitiless, sent by Aphrodite—Love
rocks and tosses my heart.

SAPPHO
OF MYTILÉNE

Sappho probably lived from about 620 to 550. We know, really, very little about her life and still less about the society in which she lived, except that it was probably not much like Athenian society. Her specialty was short lyrics, for a single reciter or private reading, in the dialect of her own country (the Aeolic of Lesbos) and in simple but superbly articulated stanzas. The famous remark of Meléager the anthologist, generally translated "few but roses all," is quite misleading even if the translation is correct, as it may not be. Sappho's lyrics were demonstrably numerous.

Of the selections given here, the third is a much-reconstructed piece. It has been doubted whether Sappho actually composed the "Epitaph for Timas."

I still treat Diehl as my main text because of wide circulation but have followed the new and better text of Lobel and Page in some places.

1 · *Invocation to Aphrodite*

Throned in splendor, deathless, O Aphrodite,
child of Zeus, charm-fashioner, I entreat you
not with griefs and bitternesses to break my
    spirit, O goddess;

standing by me rather, if once before now
far away you heard, when I called upon you,
left your father's dwelling place and descended,
    yoking the golden

chariot to sparrows, who fairly drew you

down in speed aslant the black world, the bright air
trembling at the heart to the pulse of countless
      fluttering wingbeats.

Swiftly then they came, and you, blessed lady,
smiling on me out of immortal beauty,
asked me what affliction was on me, why I
      called thus upon you,

what beyond all else I would have befall my
tortured heart: "Whom then would you have Per-
      suasion
force to serve desire in your heart? Who is it,
      Sappho, that hurt you?

Though she now escape you, she soon will follow;
though she take not gifts from you, she will give
      them:
though she love not, yet she will surely love you
      even unwilling."

In such guise come even again and set me
free from doubt and sorrow; accomplish all those
things my heart desires to be done; appear and
      stand at my shoulder.

· 2 ·

Like the very gods in my sight is he who
sits where he can look in your eyes, who listens
close to you, to hear the soft voice, its sweetness
      murmur in love and

laughter, all for him. But it breaks my spirit;
underneath my breast all the heart is shaken.
Let me only glance where you are, the voice dies,
      I can say nothing,

but my lips are stricken to silence, under-
neath my skin the tenuous flame suffuses;
nothing shows in front of my eyes, my ears are
      muted in thunder.

And the sweat breaks running upon me, fever
shakes my body, paler I turn than grass is;
I can feel that I have been changed, I feel that
    death has come near me.

· 3 ·

Some there are who say that the fairest thing seen
on the black earth is an array of horsemen;
some, men marching; some would say ships; but I say
    she whom one loves best

is the loveliest. Light were the work to make this
plain to all, since she, who surpassed in beauty
all mortality, Helen, once forsaking
    her lordly husband,

fled away to Troy-land across the water.
Not the thought of child nor beloved parents
was remembered, after the Queen of Cyprus
    won her at first sight.

Since young brides have hearts that can be persuaded
easily, light things, palpitant to passion
as am I, remembering Anaktória
    who has gone from me

and whose lovely walk and the shining pallor
of her face I would rather see before my
eyes than Lydia's chariots in all their glory
    armored for battle.

· 4 ·

Come to me from Crete to this holy temple,
Aphrodite. Here is a grove of apple
trees for your delight, and the smoking altars
    fragrant with incense.

Here cold water rustles down through the apple
branches; all the lawn is beset and darkened

under roses, and, from the leaves that tremble,
    sleep of enchantment

comes descending. Here is a meadow pasture
where the horses graze and with flowers of springtime
now in blossom, here where the light winds passing
    blow in their freshness.

Here in this place, lady of Cyprus, lightly
lifting, lightly pour in the golden goblets
as for those who keep a festival, nectar:
    wine for our drinking.

5 · *To a Rival*

You will die and be still, never shall be memory left of you
after this, nor regret when you are gone. You have not touched the
    flowers
of the Muses, and thus, shadowy still in the domain of Death,
you must drift with a ghost's fluttering wings, one of the darkened
    dead.

· 6 ·

But I claim there will be some who remember us when we are gone.

· 7 ·

When we lived all as one, she adored you as
symbol of some divinity,
    Arignóta, delighted in your dancing.

Now she shines among Lydian women as
into dark when the sun has set
    the moon, pale-handed, at last appeareth

making dim all the rest of the stars, and light
spreads afar on the deep, salt sea,
    spreading likewise across the flowering cornfields;

and the dew rinses glittering from the sky;
roses spread, and the delicate
    antherisk, and the lotus spreads her petals.

So she goes to and fro there, remembering
Atthis and her compassion, sick
the tender mind, and the heart with grief is eaten.

· 8 ·

Like the sweet apple turning red on the branch top, on the
top of the topmost branch, and the gatherers did not notice it,
rather, they did notice, but could not reach up to take it.

Like the hyacinth in the hills which the shepherd people
step on, trampling into the ground the flower in its purple.

9 · *Epitaph*

This is the dust of Timas, who died before she was married
and whom Persephone's dark chamber accepted instead.
After her death the maidens who were her friends, with sharp iron
cutting their lovely hair, laid it upon her tomb.

ALCAÉUS
OF MYTILÉNE

Alcaéus was a fellow countryman and contemporary of Sappho and lived a
stormy youth as an aristocrat, first fighting tyranny, then resisting social re-
form, in his city. Politically, he seems to represent one kind of group Solon
had to contend with; and Píttakos, for a time the archenemy of Alcaéus, was
quite possibly Solon's exemplar and certainly his counterpart. Vigorous, brave,
and opinionated, Alcaéus, who wrote so much political poetry, shows in his
extant work no constructive political sense whatever. As a craftsman in verse,
nevertheless, he rivals Sappho at her best.

Reconsideration of the text and of the work of Lobel and Page has led me
to make a few revisions.

1 · *Storm in the State*

I cannot understand how the winds are set
against each other. Now from this side and now

from that the waves roll. We between them
   run with the wind in our black ship driven,

hard pressed and laboring under the giant storm.
All round the mast-step washes the sea we shipped.
   You can see through the sail already
     where there are opening rents within it.

The forestays slacken. . . .

*social
unrest*

2 · *Prayer for Safety at Sea*

Be with me now, leaving the Isle of Pelops,
mighty sons of Zeus and of Leda, now in
kindliness of heart appear to me, Kastor
     and Polydeúkes:

you who wander over the wide earth, over
all the sea's domain on your flying horses,
easily delivering mortal men from
     death and its terror:

swept in far descent to the strong-built vessel's
masthead, you ride shining upon the cables,
through the weariness of the dark night bringing
     light to the black ship.

· 3 ·

Hebros, loveliest of rivers, you issue
hard by Ainos into the dark blue waters
of the sea where, passing by Thrace, you end your
     turbulent passage;

there where young girls come in their crowds and, bathing
with light hands their ravishing thighs, enjoy you
all as if some magical salve were in your
     wonderful waters.

4 · *Winter Scene*

Zeus rains upon us, and from the sky comes down
enormous winter. Rivers have turned to ice. . . .

Dash down the winter. Throw a log on the fire
and mix the flattering wine (do not water it
    too much) and bind on round our foreheads
      soft ceremonial wreaths of spun fleece.

We must not let our spirits give way to grief.
By being sorry we get no further on,
    my Bukchis. Best of all defenses
      is to mix plenty of wine, and drink it.

· 5 ·

Wet your whistle with wine now, for the dog star, wheeling up the
    sky,
brings back summer, the time all things are parched under the sear-
    ing heat.
Now the cicada's cry, sweet in the leaves, shrills from beneath his
    wings.
Now the artichoke flowers, women are lush, ask too much of their
    men,
who grow lank, for the star burning above withers their brains and
    knees.

· 6 ·

This was the word of Aristodámos in Sparta, and not so badly phrased
    at all.
He said: "Money's the man." It's true. There's no poor man who's
    known as good or valued much.

7 · *The Armory*

The great hall is aglare with bronze armament and the whole inside
    made fit for war

with helms glittering and hung high, crested over with white horse-
    manes that nod and wave
and make splendid the heads of men who wear them. Here are shin-
    ing greaves made out of bronze,
hung on hooks, and they cover all the house's side. They are strong
    to stop arrows and spears.
Here are war-jackets quilted close of new linen, with hollow shields
    stacked on the floor,
with broad swords of the Chalkis make, many tunics and many belts
    heaped close beside.
These shall not lie neglected, now we have stood to our task and have
    this work to do.

ANÁCREON
OF TEOS

Apparently Anácreon lived from about 560 to 490 B.C. Driven from Teos,
his home in Asia Minor, by the Persian inroad, he settled with his country-
men in Thrace and later pursued a career as a professional poet. Late in life he
arrived at Athens, probably ended his days there, and seems to have influenced
the young Aeschylus, who used some of his meters. In fact, though there is no
reason to think that Anácreon himself wrote tragedy, his metrical influence
on Attic tragedy may have been very great indeed, perhaps decisive; but this
feeling of mine rests on inference rather than positive statement and remains
a feeling.

His own surviving work seems, indeed, less important than his effects on
others, though these effects were partly accidental. The far later, anonymous
Anacreóntea, lyrics which were never meant to pass as anything but frank imi-
tations of Anácreon, had an immense influence on the lyric of the Renaissance
in France and England.

· 1 ·

The love god with his golden curls
puts a bright ball into my hand,
shows a girl in her fancy shoes,
    and suggests that I take her.

Not that girl—she's the other kind,
one from Lesbos. Disdainfully,
nose turned up at my silver hair,
she makes eyes at the ladies.

· 2 ·

Once he went out huddled about in dirty clothes with his hair skimped
up,
buttons of wood hung in his ears for rings, and the hide of a thread-
bare ox
scrubbed from a cast-off shield to wrap
his bones to keep him warm. For friends all he could get was pastry
cooks
or girls who walked the streets for fun. He was the lousy Ártemon.
He lived the life of a useless bum.
He got his neck framed in the pillory, he got whipped till his back
was raw,
he had hairs pulled out of his head.
Look at him now, Kýkē's boy; he rides in a coach and four, and wears
gold on his arms, gold on his neck, shaded by ivory parasols,
like some dame in society.

· 3 ·

Like a blacksmith the Love God has hammered me and crushed me
on his anvil, and has plunged me in a winter torrent.

· 4 ·

Altogether like a young fawn dropped but lately,
still a nurseling, who has lost her antlered mother
in the forest, and is overcome with panic.

· 5 ·

I have gone gray at the temples,
yes, my head is white, there's nothing
of the grace of youth that's left me,
and my teeth are like an old man's.

Life is lovely. But the lifetime
that remains for me is little.
For this cause I mourn. The terrors
of the Dark Pit never leave me.
For the house of Death is deep down
underneath; the downward journey
to be feared, for once I go there
I know well there's no returning.

ANONYMOUS DRINKING SONGS

At the *symposium* or drinking party in Athens and probably elsewhere too, it was customary for the guests to sing songs, at first as a group, then individually (*scólia*). Sometimes the works of known poets were sung; Alcaéus, Anácreon, Simónides, and Praxílla are among those mentioned. Sometimes, again, the guests improvised, line by line or stanza by stanza, preserving the meter. A number of such improvisations, originating in sixth-century Athens, then seem to have become more or less canonized and were repeated again and again. A collection of these is preserved in the *Deipnosophístae* of Athenaéus, 15. 694–95.

Subjects were various: praise of gods and of heroes, moral maxims, and sometimes comments on political issues. All this could also be said of the works of Alcaéus, one of whose poems has got into the Anonymous-Attic collection. The stanza, however, not the whole poem, appears to be the unit; and thus the lines to Harmódios and Aristogeíton form not one poem but a series of stanzas in honor of the famous pair who "liberated Athens" (actually they did not) by killing Hippárchos, brother of the tyrant Híppias, in 514 B.C. This, at least, appears to be the case, but it has also been ascribed to one Callístratus, as if it were a regular poem.

· 1 ·

I will wear my sword in a spray of myrtle
like Harmódios and Aristogeíton
when they killed the usurper and made
Athens be once again a city where all are free.

Dear Harmódios, surely you have not perished.
No, they say, you live in the blessed islands
where Achilles, the swift of foot,
and Tydeus' son, Diomedes, are said to have gone.

I will wear my sword in a spray of myrtle
like Harmódios and Aristogeíton
when at Athene's processional
they killed Hippárchos, the man who had usurped
    the power.

Always your fame shall live with us forever,
dear Harmódios and Aristogeíton,
since you killed the usurper and made
Athens be once again a city where all are free.

tyrant

· 2 ·

He who never betrays one he has made a friend shall be given high
exaltation among people and gods. Such is my own belief.

· 3 ·

Oh that it were given to us to open
up the heart of every man, and to read his
mind within, and then to close it,
and thus, never deceived, be assured of a friend.

· 4 ·

Underneath every stone there lies hidden a scorpion, dear friend.
Take care, or he will sting you. All concealment is treachery.

HÝBRIAS
OF CRETE

The *scólium* here translated is given by Athenaéus as an appendix to the
collection of Attic drinking songs. Nothing is known about the author. His
name, which is perhaps best translated "Bully," seems almost too good to be
true.

My wealth is great; it is a spear and a sword, *wealth*
and the grand hairy shield to guard my body.
With these I plow, with these I harvest,
with these I tread the sweet wine from the grapevine,
with these I am called master of the rabble.

And they who dare not carry the spear and sword
and the grand hairy shield to guard their bodies,
all these fall down before me, kiss my knee, hail me
their high king and master. *tyrant*

PRAXÍLLA
OF SÍCYON

Praxílla is placed as being "well known" in the middle of the fifth century and is thus later than the other poets included in this selection. The two scraps here given are like nothing else in early Greek poetry. The love of simple things shown in the first fragment was not always understood, nor well received. "Sillier than Praxílla's Adónis" was a proverb, it seems, because Adónis, the speaker of these lines, mentioned cucumbers along with the sun and moon. Enough said.

· 1 ·

Loveliest of what I leave behind is the sunlight,
and loveliest after that the shining stars, and the moon's face,
but also cucumbers that are ripe, and pears, and apples.

· 2 ·

Girl of the lovely glance, looking out through the window,
your face is virgin; lower down you are a married woman.

ANONYMOUS LYRICS

There are, in addition to the *scólia* and the inscribed epigrams, a number of anonymous early poems (*carmina popularia*) preserved in whole or in part. They are often called "folk songs," but this term seems strangely misleading. I give only three very short poems which could be regarded as complete. The second is often attributed to Sappho.

1 · (*Lesbos*)

Grind on millstone, grind on,
for even Píttakos grinds on,
and he's king over mighty Mytiléne.

tyrant

2 · (*Lesbos*)

The moon has gone down, the Pleiades
have set; and the night's at halfway,
and the time is passing,
and I lie in my bed, lonely.

3 · (*Locris*)

Oh what ails you? Do not betray me, I implore you.
Before he comes back, get up, never ruin
yourself, do not ruin me a poor wretched sinner.
It is day now, see the light through the window, do you
    not see it?

CORÍNNA
OF TÁNAGRA

Corínna was a contemporary of Pindar and might therefore have lived in the last part of the sixth and the first part of the fifth centuries. This early date has, however, been questioned by Page and others. She also counts practically as Pindar's compatriot, since Thebes and Tánagra were members of the same Boeótian League; and she is said to have competed against Pindar, despite her criticism of Myrtis (4) for doing just that, and to have criticized and counseled him (see Pindar 2). But her work and her career are quite different from Pindar's. Being a woman, she seems to have confined herself to her home territory, and so she uses her own vernacular instead of the international literary-Doric of the great traveling poet. There is something quaint and parochial, not to say unfinished, about her work, though metrically, to the distress of modern critics, she seems to be the exemplar for certain schemes of Attic Tragedy.

Asópos (2) was a river in Boeótia, and his daughters were supposed to include Aegína, Tánagra, Thebe, Sinópe, Corcýra, and other such local heroine-goddesses, but our fragment is not in shape to clinch such information. Kithaíron and Hélikon (3) were mountains, here personified.

· 1 ·

To the white-mantled maidens
of Tánagra I sing my sweet lays.
I am the pride of my city
for my conversational singing.

2 · *The Daughters of Asópos*

. . . Of your daughters, our Father Zeus
king over all, possesses three;
Poseídon, governor of the great
main, wed three; and of yet two more
Apollo is lord and lover.

One has gone to Hermes, strong child
of Maia. This was the urge of Love
and the lady of Cyprus, that these gods
secretly enter your house, and take
possession of your nine daughters.

In their time the girls shall give birth
to a hero race, half-divine.
They shall be ageless and bear children.
So from my tripod oracular
I proclaim.

Such the privilege I maintain,
one out of fifty brothers, strong

men, but I supreme, ordained
prophet of secret mysteries
without falsehood, Akraíphen.

On Euónymos first of all
Leto's son bestowed the speaking
of oracles from his own tripod.
Hýrieus, driving him from the land,
held the privilege, second

he, and Poseídon's son, and next
Oríon, our own father, who won
back the land that had been his own.
He has his place now in the sky.
Now I hold this privilege.

3 · *The Contest of Kithaíron and Hélikon*

The Kourétes
nursed the goddess' holy child
in the cave, in secrecy from
devious-devising Kronos
when blessed Rheia stole him away;

and he, Zeus, took the high degree
among the immortals. This was his song.
The Muses told the high gods then
each to deposit his ballot stone
secretly in the gold gleaming
urns. Together the gods rose up.

Kithaíron won more of the votes.
At once Hermes, with a great cry,
announced him, how he had gained success
he longed for, and the blessed gods
with garlands crowned him, so that his heart
was happy.

But Hélikon, in his rage and pain,
tore a stone from the mountainside
and in his sorrow dashed it down
from high, into a thousand shards.

· 4 ·

I disapprove even of eloquent
Myrtis; I do, for she, a woman,
contended with Pindar.

SIMÓNIDES
OF CEOS

Simónides is thought to have lived from about 556 to about 468 B.C. He was
a widely traveled and widely known professional poet; at home in both
Athens and Sparta, friend alike of Themístocles and Pausánias; and above all,
the voice of the Pan-Hellenic resistance against the great invasion of Xerxes
in 480 B.C. He was one of the wisest of the early Greek poets. Certainly, he
was the most versatile of all and was master of practically every form then
known. He wrote elegies ranging in length from the two-line epigram, to be
inscribed, to extensive historical narrative in elegiac verse. He wrote both
lyric monodies and large choral compositions and developed the victory ode,
anticipating Pindar as well as his own nephew Bacchýlides. He is even said
to have written tragedies.

Nevertheless, the most famous poem ascribed to him, the epitaph for the
Spartans who died fighting at Thermópylae (9), is not certainly his. The
seventh is also doubtful.

Two statements about poetry are attributed to him. They probably ap-
peared in his poems, but we have them only in paraphrase. He said: "The
word is the image of the thing." He also said that painting is silent poetry and
poetry is painting that speaks.

1 · *Danae and Perseus*

. . . when in the wrought chest
the wind blowing over
and the sea heaving
struck her with fear, her cheeks not dry,
she put her arm over Perseus and spoke: My child
such trouble I have.
And you sleep, your heart is placid;
you dream in the joyless wood;
in the night nailed in bronze,

in the blue dark you lie still and shine.
The salt water that towers above your head
as the wave goes by you
heed not, nor the wind's voice; you press
your bright face to the red blanket.
If this danger were danger to you,
your small ear would attend my words.
But I tell you: Sleep, my baby, and let the sea sleep, let
our trouble sleep; let some change appear

Zeus father, from you.
This bold word and beyond justice
I speak, I pray you, forgive it me.

2 · *Comment on a Poem of Cleobúlus*

The Epitaph of Cleobúlus

I am the maiden in bronze set over the tomb of Midas.
As long as water runs from wellsprings, and tall trees burgeon,
and the sun goes up the sky to shine, and the moon is brilliant,
as long as rivers shall flow and the wash of the sea's breakers,
so long remaining in my place on this tomb where the tears fall
I shall tell those who pass that Midas here lies buried.

The Comment of Simónides

Who that trusts his mind could believe the man of Lindos, Cleobúlus,
who against the forever flow of rivers, the spring flowers,
against sun's flame and moon gold
and the tossing of the sea, sets up the strength of a gravestone?
All things are less than the gods. That stone
even a man's hand could smash. This is the word of a fool.

· 3 ·

Being no more than a man, you cannot tell what will happen tomor-
    row,
nor, when you see one walk in prosperity know for how much time
    it will be.
For overturn on the light-lifting wings of a dragonfly
is not more swift.

· 4 ·

Not even those who lived long ago before us
and were sons of our lords, the gods, themselves half-divine,
came to an old age and the end of their days
without hardship and danger, nor did they live forever.

· 5 ·

There is one story
that Virtue has her dwelling place above rock walls hard to climb
with a grave chorus of light-footed nymphs attendant about her,
and she is not to be looked upon by the eyes of every mortal,
only by one who with sweat, with clenched concentration
and courage, climbs to the peak.

· 6 ·

To be a good man, without blame and without question,
foursquare founded hand and foot, mind also
faultless fashioned, is difficult.

Thus the word of Píttakos, but it does not
run right, though it was a wise man who said it:
that it is difficult to be excellent. Not difficult;
only a god could have this privilege; it is not *possible*
for a man not to go bad
when he has more bad luck than he can handle.
Any man is good while his luck is good,
bad when bad, and for the most part they are best
whom the gods love.

Therefore, I will not throw away my time and life
into unprofitable hope and emptiness, the search
for that object which cannot possibly be,
the Utterly Blameless Man among all of us who enjoy
man's food on the wide earth.
But if I find one, I will let you know.
No, I admire all, am a friend of any
who of his own will does nothing shameful. Against
necessity not even the gods can fight.

I do not like to find fault.
Enough for me if one is not
bad, not too unsteady, knows
what is right and good for his city,
a sound man. I will not
look out his faults. For the generation
of fools is endless. Take anything as good
which is not soiled with shame.

· 7 ·

Across the pale stillness
of water keel-carven, these lovely eyes of desire
drag the ship to her doom.

· 8 ·

As when in the winter moons God stills
weather a space of fourteen days,
and winds sleep in the season, and men have named it
sacred to the breeding of the bright halcyon.

INSCRIBED EPITAPHS

· 9 ·

Traveler, take this word to the men of Lakedaímon:
We who lie buried here did what they told us to do.

· 10 ·

This is the grave of that Megístias, whom once the Persians
and Medes killed when they crossed Spercheíos River; a seer
who saw clearly the spirits of death advancing upon him,
yet could not bring himself to desert the Spartiate kings.

· 11 ·

Friend, we once were alive in the harbor city of Korinth.
Now the island city of Salamis is our grave.

PINDAR

OF THEBES

I have added some of the more substantial or interesting items from Pindar's extensive fragments. I would now prefer 522 or even 526 for his birth date; 518 is usually accepted. He died at some time after 446 B.C. Pindar's work was all in the form of choral lyric, but some pieces may not have been intended for choral presentation. The poems were ultimately collected in seventeen books. Four books of victory odes have survived in manuscript form. Of these, the book of *Ísthmian Odes* is incomplete, and we have only the opening of the Ninth *Ísthmian*, given here as Fragment 1.

Pindar would be notable on the strength of his fragments alone, but fragments can never show him at his best. The architecture of the full ode is something never equaled, never, for that matter, approached, in all literature; lacking that, no matter how fine the individual image, we get less than half an idea of what Pindar can do. On the other hand, these fragments show many flashes of original thought, of humanity and generosity, which are sometimes thought to be wanting in the victory odes.

Fragment 2 is quoted by Plutarch in connection with an anecdote. Corínna is said to have lectured him for his failure to use myth, and when Pindar wrote the opening of a poem which begins with our text, Corínna laughed and told him he should sow with the hand, not with the whole sack. The Paean for the people of Ceos (4) is Boeótian in its personification of places (see Corínna 3). The account of Neoptólemos (5) gave great offense to the Aeginétan friends of Pindar, who counted that hero as one of their own protective Aiákidai; and his apology contains the explanation for much previously obscure matter in the *Seventh Némean*.

1 · *The Ninth Ísthmian Ode*

Glorious is the legend of Aíakos, glorious the fame by sea of
    Aigína. By the gods' good will
the Dorian host of Hyllos
and Aigímios, there arriving,
founded her; by their standards administered
her people live, transgressing
no right nor privilege of strangers; for active achievement
they are dolphins in the sea: accomplished dispensers
of the Muses, and the games' endeavors.

· 2 ·

Shall it be Isménos, or Mélia of the golden distaff,
or Kadmos, or the sacred generation of Sown Men,
or Thebe of the dark blue veil,
or the dare-all strength of Herakles,
or the gracious cult of Dionýsos,
or the marriage of white-armed Harmónia? Which shall we sing?

· 3 ·

First of all, on a golden chariot beside the well-springs
of Ocean, the goddesses of Destiny brought the counselor, heavenly
Themis, to the hallowed stairway
that leads by a shining way to Olympos,
there to be the primeval wife of Zeus the Savior.
And she bore him the shining-veiled, the bright-with-fruit
Seasons, goddesses of Truth.

4 · *Paean for the People of Keos*

As for me, though I live on a rock, I am distinguished for achievement
in the games of the Hellenes, and I am known
well enough for the Muse.
If also my lands yield something
of Dionýsos' life-giving medicine against despair,
yet I have no horses, no part in the cattle ranges.
Yet Melámpos, once, was unwilling
to leave his own country and be a king in Argos,
once he had established his prophetic position.
Ié, ié, o ié paían.

What is near home, city and hearth
and kinship, this gives a man something to stay
and love, and the passion for what is far away
belongs to vain fools. I accept the word of the lord,
Euxántios, when the men of Crete wooed him and he refused
to be a king, and among their hundred cities hold
the seventh part with the sons of Pasíphaë,
and spoke to them of a portent, and made it his:
"I fear the assault of Zeus, I fear the Earthshaker and his heavy stroke.

These once, with thunderbolt and trident,
overwhelmed the earth and the host altogether
of mankind into deep Tártaros, leaving
my mother, Keos, and all her house intact.
Then shall I, striving for riches, thrust aside
all the established worship of the Blessed Ones into desolation
while I hold a great grant elsewhere?
Terror would be too much a thing always with me.
Let the cypress go, my heart, let go the ranges of Ida."

Thin is the soil given me, so I am treeless, but labors nor quarrels are
      my inheritance.

5 · *Paean for the Délphians*

The god of the far cast,
in mortal guise of Paris,
struck down Achílleus; so made to come
later the fall of Ílion

when he, strong wall of the Achaíans, child
violent of dark-haired Thetis of the sea, was stopped
in brute death, by the God
who shouldered his own stark strength against Hera
of the white arms, against Athene lady of citadels. Else these men had
      stormed
the Dardánian city without great labor, had not Apollo guarded it.
But he who sits among the peaks and the golden snows of Olympos,
Zeus, gods' guard, had no heart
to break destiny. For the sake of deep-haired Helen
wide Pérgamon had to go down in the searing blaze of the fire.
      As the powerful
body of Péleus' son was laid with mourning to burn on the pyre,
messengers returned over the swell of the waters, bringing
from Skyros back
in all his strength Neoptólemos

who sacked Ílion city.
But he, too, was never to come back into the sight
of his gracious mother, nor in his father's acres

quicken the bronze-helmed host
of the Mýrmidon riders to battle.
Near Tómaros in the land of Molóssia he made
his landfall, neither got clear of the stormwinds
nor of him who strikes afar from a broad quiver. For the god had
    sworn
that Neoptólemos, who struck down aged
Priam as he stood on the protecting altar, should come to no kind
    home,
nor live into old age; and as he fought with the god's ministers
for high honor of place, Apollo killed him
there, in the beloved precinct, beside the great centerstone of the
    earth.

6 · *Paean for the Thebans*
After the Solar Eclipse of 463 B.C.

Beam-of-the-sun, what far-reaching thing have you intended,
O Mother of Sights, that the highest star of all
be hooded in daytime? Why have you made helpless
men's strength, and the way of wisdom,
as you run along a course which is darkened?
Do you drive into being some new thing not known before?
In the name of Zeus, O guider of swift horses,
I implore you, steer
toward some blessing and no harm for Thebes,
lady, this portent that is there for all.

. . . .

Do you bring some blazon of war;
punishment of seed; power of snow
beyond imagination; malignant inward dissension;
or the great sea emptied out upon the plain;
freezing of the earth, or wet heat
running in wrath of water;
or will you wash down the whole world, and make
a new generation from the beginning?

I make no outcry over what I will suffer with all the rest.

. . . .

By something more than mortal I have been marked
near by the ambrosial bed of Mélia
to bring together the proud sound in the reed
with the imagination in my heart for your grace and hers.
Lord of the far cast, I pray to you;
I have dedicated to the artistry of the Muses
your oracle, Apollo,

where long ago, Pythian, the young daughter of Ocean,
Mélia, bride of your bed, gave birth to strong
Téneros, high prophet of your decrees.
To him, for his sober courage,
father, you of the unshorn hair, you entrusted
the host of Kadmos and the city of Zethos, Thebes.
And the Trident-wielder of the sea likewise
favored him beyond men beside,
and for his sake pinched together the Channel.

7 · *Athens*

O shining and wreathed in violets, city of singing,
stanchion of Hellas, glorious Athens,
citadel full of divinity.

8 · *Sparta*

There the elders' councils
are best, the spears of the young men,
the choral grace, the Muse.

· 9 ·

War is sweet to those who have not tried it. The experienced
man is frightened at the heart to see it advancing.

· 10 ·

Let one who has brought the commonwealth
to calm peace, search then
for the light, the shining of great-hearted Concord,

and drive malignant Discord away from his mind,
bestower of poverty, spiteful as nurse of children.

· 11 ·

O Thrasyboúlos, I send this gear of racing and lovely
songs to you for the end of your revels. So may you share it
with them who drink beside you, sweet instigator to them,
    to the yield

of Dionýsos' abundance and the flagons of Athens
at that time of night when the troublesome cares of humanity
drift from our hearts and on seas of luxury streaming in gold

we swim together, and make for a shore that is nowhere.
The poor man now is rich. . . .

12 · *The Blessed Dead*

On them is lit the strength of the sun beneath the darkness we know
    here,
and the space before the city of them lies in bright-flowering meadows,
shadowy with incense-trees and heavy with golden fruits.
And some with horses and exercise, some with draughts-games,
some with lyres take their pleasure, and a whole life of bliss breaks
    into flower upon them.
A lovely fragrance is scattered across the place
as they join all manner of sacrifices to bright fire on the gods' altars.

There the torpid rivers of the gloom of night
break through the endless dark.

· 13 ·

For all creatures the body goes the way of Death in his strength,
but there is still left a living image of the life. This alone
comes from the gods. It sleeps in the action of the limbs, but as we
    sleep in dream after dream
it shows the judgment between pleasures and hardships advancing
    upon us.

· 14 ·

Blessèd is he who has seen these things and goes under the ground.
He knows life's end.
He knows the empire given by the God.

· 15 ·

Those from whom Perséphone accepts compensation for an old
sorrow, in the ninth year she renders up their souls again
to the upper sunlight; from such souls grow proud kings,
men quick in their strength, men supreme
for wisdom, and into the rest of time these are called holy heroes
among mankind.

· 16 ·

Do not against all comers let break the word that is not needed.
There are times when the way of silence is best; the word in its power
can be the spur to battle.

· 17 ·

Mistress of high achievement, O lady Truth,
do not let my understanding stumble
across some jagged falsehood.

BACCHÝLIDES
OF CEOS

Bacchýlides was the nephew (sister's son) of Simónides and therefore
presumably about of an age with Pindar, against whom he competed, success-
fully on the whole, though there is an inescapable feeling, for me at least, that
he mostly followed where Pindar led the way. The first two poems are dithy-
rambs or dramatic lyrics; the others, victory odes. Of these, again, the third
is dated to 476 B.C., for the same occasion as Pindar's *First Olympian*. The
fourth celebrates the four-horse-chariot victory which Hieron finally succeed-
ed in winning in 468 B.C., when, it seems, he commissioned Bacchýlides but

not Pindar. The date of the fifth, for a young victor from Metapóntion in Italy, is not known.

The most puzzling narrative is, perhaps, in the second dithyramb. It deals with a familiar story, that of Theseus and the seven young men and seven girls sent from Athens as tribute to Crete. But instead of telling the story in full, Bacchýlides finds himself concentrating on a single incident. Theseus and the Fourteen are bound for Crete, and King Minos himself is on board. The arrogant Minos publicly makes advances to Eriboía, one of the girls; Theseus steps between and challenges him. Minos has claimed to be the son of Zeus; Theseus, of Poseídon. Minos appeals to Zeus to confirm his fathership by a thunderflash, which he does; then Minos dares Theseus to prove that Poseídon of the sea acknowledges him, by throwing his ring overboard and challenging Theseus to go down and recover it. Theseus does so; and there Bacchýlides simply ends his story.

For restorations to fill out the text of Bacchýlides, I am indebted to the editions of Blass, Jebb, Kenyon, Snell, and particularly Edmonds. I also take this occasion to acknowledge my gratitude to the great company of true scholars who have collected, edited, pieced out, and interpreted all the texts which have been used in these translations.

1 · *The Coming of Theseus: A Dithyramb*

Chorus with leader

King of Athens, the sacred city,
lord of luxurious Ionians,
what news of war is this that the trumpet's
bronze-belled braying call announces?
Is it some enemy war captain
overstriding our land's boundaries
with his own host at heel?
Is it robbers, whose ways are evil,
overcoming our shepherds' resistance,
driving our flocks away?
What is it that gnaws at your heart?
Tell us; for I think, if any man
has the strong support of hard-fighting
men-at-arms, it is you,
O son of Pandíon and Kreoúsa, Aígeus.

King of Athens

A messenger has come in, completing
the long run between here and the Isthmus,
telling of deeds incredible done by
a strong man. He has killed overpowering
Sinis, once the greatest in strength
of men, being son to Kronid Lytaíos
(earthshaker, that is, Poseidon);
killed, too, the manslaughtering wild boar
in the valley of Krémmyon, and killed
wicked and cruel Skiron.
He has abolished the wrestling-ring
of Kérkyon. The Pounder has dropped
Polypémon's strong hammer from hand.
He met with a better man. I fear
this news. I do not know what it all may come to.

Chorus with leader

Who is this hero, then, does he say?
Where does he come from? What has he with him?
Does he come armed with weapons of war?
Has he a great following behind him?
Or alone, and with body servants
only, goes he as a merchant who travels
into alien lands?
Strong he must be, and resolute,
adventurous, too, who has stood the onset
of such big men and put them down.
Surely, the drive of a god is behind him,
to bring law to the lawless people.
It is no easy thing to engage
again and again, and never be loser.
In the length of time all things are brought to com-
     pletion.

King of Athens

The man says only two attendants
go with him. On his gleaming shoulders

he wears a sword with an ivory hilt;
two polished throwing-spears in his hands;
a well-wrought skin-cap of Sparta
covers his head and his bright hair;
over his chest a sea-dyed
shirt, and, above, a Thessalian
cloak of frieze. In his eyes there shines
the flamelight of a Lemnos
volcano. Yet he is said to be
a boy, in his first youth, but a boy
trained to feel the finesse of war
and bronze-battering Ares' work.
The end of his search is said to be shining Athens.

2 · *Theseus and the Ring: A Dithyramb*

A dark-prowed ship, carrying battle-brave
Theseus and twice seven glorious Ionian
young men and maidens,
was cutting the open sea off Crete,
for into her sails far-white-gleaming
blew the northerly winds
by grace of renowned Athene, she of the battle-aegis;
but the dangerous gifts of the Cyprian
goddess, who wears the veil of desire,
stung in the heart of Minos,
and he could not keep his hand from the girl
longer, but laid it upon her cheek,
and she, Eriboía, screamed
for the bronze-armored Pandíonid
Theseus, who gave him a black
and rolling eye from under brows,
and in him the pain of rage
clawed the heart, and he spoke:
"O son of lordliest Zeus, here
is no proper spirit now
that you steer in the inward heart.
Hero, control that grasping violence.

That which powerful destiny from the gods
has nodded our way, and as the scale-beam of Justice
dips, such will be the provided
course that we shall fill out whenever
it comes. You keep that heavy design
in control. Even if you are son
born to the bed of Zeus under the brow of Mount Ida
from the handsomely named daughter
of Phoinix, so among mortals
most high; yet I also myself
come from the daughter of wealthy Píttheus
when she lay with the lord of the sea,
Poseídon; and the violet-wreathed
daughters of Néreus gave her
a veil of gold. Therefore,
O war captain of the Knóssians,
I tell you, hold in check your lust;
much hurt it can do, for I would not
consent to look on the glorious light
of ambrosial dawn, were you to force
any of these youths or maidens
unwilling; sooner we shall show down the strength
of our hands, and what comes of it the gods will decide."

So much spoke the spear-brave hero,
and the seafarers stood dumb-struck
at the overtowering audacity
of the man, and Hélios' son-in-law was angered at heart,
and began the weaving of a stratagem
that would surprise, and he spoke: "Zeus, huge
of strength, Father, hear me. If Phoinix' daughter,
your white-armed bride, bore me your son,
now grant me out of the sky a rapid
fire-haired thunderflash, a sign
conspicuous; you, also,
if Aithra of Troizen truly bore you
son to Poseídon the earth shaker,
here is this golden
finger-ornament,

my ring; fetch it me out of the deep of the sea;
be bold, dive in, down to your father's house.
So shall you know if the Kronian
lord of the thunder-
stroke, master of all, hears my prayers."

And Zeus great of strength listened to the prayers
without fault, and planted a high portent,
wishing to make his son's
place of honor clear in all eyes;
and he flashed lightning. Minos, seeing
the welcome portent, lifted his arms
into the resounding sky, he, battle-brave hero,
and spoke: "Theseus, here
are my gifts from Zeus, plain for your eyes
to see. Dive then into the deep-
humming sea, and the son of Kronos
your father, the lord Poseídon,
will give you the highest glory
over all the earth well-grown with trees."
He spoke, and the heart in the other
did not twist away; standing
high on the well-planked deck,
he sprang, and friendly the sea-forest
gathered him down. Zeus' son
Minos, in inward amazement
of heart, gave order to hold the elaborate
ship down wind and away.
But Destiny pushed on another course.

And the fast-faring hull went, and the north
wind blew from astern and scudded her on,
and all the group of the youth
from Athens trembled, now
that their hero had taken the sea-plunge.
From their soft eyes they shed tears,
and looked for a hard pass and heavy to be brought to.
But the sea-people, the dolphins,
nimbly carried tall Theseus

to the house of his horseman father.
He came into the gods' palace.
There looking about him in fear
he saw the fabulous daughters
of rich Néreus, and from their glorious
bodies the light glanced shimmering
as of flame, and on their locks were circled
gold-implicated
ribbons, as they refreshed their hearts
with dancing, lithe-footed.
He looked on the stately true wife of his father
in that alluring house,
Amphitríte the ox-eyed,
who cast about him a robe, purple with sea-dye,

and laid upon the curls of his hair
the wreath, unflawed,
that once at her own marriage
beguiling Aphrodíte rose-crowned had given her.
For men of close counsel
nothing the gods accomplish passes belief.
Beside the slim stern of the ship he came up, and ah
in what thoughts he bewildered the lord
of the armies of Knossos, now
coming out dry from the sea,
a wonder to all, and over
his body gleamed the gift of the gods, and the bright-
throned nymphs, in new found
hilarity raised the high scream
of triumph,
and the sea echoed, the youths about him
sang with voice of love and acclaim.
Delian, lord, your own heart softened
by the chorales of the Keans,
grant a god-sped happening of success.

3 · *Olympian Ode for Híeron* (*Horse Race*)

High lord and leader of men
in Syracuse of the dashing horses,
you shall be judge of this work
of art, this gift of the violet-wreathed Muses, you,
if any man on earth,
can read it. Rest then that just
mind, stilled now, undisturbed by troubles,
turn our way your deep attention,
if by consent of the deep-waisted goddesses of Grace
your far friend in his sacred
island fashioned and sent
to your famous city this song
which he, a great servant of gold-veiled
Urania, made. His wish is
that the voice spring from within him

in praise of Híeron. Shearing
the deep sky with his golden pinions
and high speed of wings,
the eagle, messenger to the wide majesty
of Zeus loud-thundering,
goes bold in his big strength, and below
the thin-screaming small birds
huddle away from him, in fear.
Not the lifted peaks of great earth are barrier,
not the harsh climbing crests
of ever heaving salt water. Out
in lone space he steers
the glossed and light plumes of his wings
and rides the west wind
to fill the eyes of men with wonder.

Like him, I too have a thousand ways to go for my
        choosing
for the song of your achievement
given by the hands of Victory, lady of the dark tresses,
by armor-chested Ares also,
you lordly sons of Deinómenes.

May the god who uses you well not weary of it.
Dawn, goddess, she of the golden arms
looked down and saw the bay horse, Pherénikos,
run like a storm by the broad
whirling waters of Alpheos river to win his race.

So too in hallowed Pytho.
I lean hand on earth and declare,
never yet have rival horses
run before him, the dust of them fouling him as he
    galloped
down the home stretch to his goal.
He goes like a gust of the north wind,
yet waits the will of his rider, to sweep
fresh victories for Híeron
and bursts of applause for that hospitable man.
Fortunate he, whom the god
has granted his share of splendors,
and, with that happiness all wish for,
to go through a prosperous lifetime: not
blessed in everything: for no man
born has fortune on his side always.

No, for there was a time,
the legends say, when even the invincible
son of white-thunder-flashing
Zeus, Herakles, went down to the dark gates of
    light-footed
Persephone, to haul up
that jag-toothed dog whom the snaky monster
spawned, from death to daylight.
There, beside the Waters of Wailing,
he was aware of the ghosts of unhappy dead men
rustling, as on the colored slopes
of Ida, where the flocks are pastured,
wind stirs the leaves. Clear showed
among them the shade of Meleágros,
Portheus' grandson, in his day a daring
man at arms with the handled spear.

Now as Alkméne's strong and glorious son saw
    Meleágros
shining in all his war gear,
he hooked the loud twanging string to the bowhorn,
then plucked a brazen-headed arrow,
flipping the quiver-lid
back. But facing him now the phantom of Meleágros
came closer, and knew him well,
and, knowing him, spoke: "Son of Zeus,
the great god, hold fast
where you are, and pacify that adventurous spirit.

Useless for you to let fly
from your hands a rasping arrow
into the ghosts of dead men.
You have nothing to fear." He spoke. Amphítryon's
    lordly
son stared at him in wonder,
answered: "What immortal god,
or was it a mortal, raised such a branch
of strength? What country could breed such?
Who could have killed you? Surely then Hera, girt in
    splendor,
will send your killer to hunt
my head too. But Pallas Athene,
the golden-haired, will be there to help me."
Then bursting into tears, Meleágros
answered him: "It is hard for men
who are mere earthly creatures to fend off

what the gods have determined to do.
Otherwise Oíneus, lasher of horses,
would have turned back the rancor of Artemis,
the white-armed, the high goddess with buds of flow-
    ers in her hair,
with supplication by abundant
sacrifice of goats and of red-backed
oxen. He was my father.

No, but
the goddess kept her anger untamed
and would not let be. The Maiden let loose a power-
   ful,
cruelly fighting wild boar
on the lordly countryside of Kalydon.
There, in swelled riptide of brute force,
he tore with tusks the poled vineyards,
slaughtered the sheep flocks and any man
who dared stand his ground against him.

Around this creature we, the chosen best out of all
   the Hellenes,
closed in and fought with a will
six whole days on end, till at last the goddess
let us men of Aitolia win.
We buried those who had gone down
before the onrush and screaming charge of the wild
   boar,
Ankaíos and with him Ageláos,
bravest of all my excellent brothers,
born in the same renowned palace
with me to Althaía and to Oíneus our father.

With these, sorrowful fate destroyed
others also. For Artemis, Leto's proud daughter,
had not yet made an end
to the cruelty of her anger, and over the warm-colored
   hide
we now fought on with a will,
we and the battling Kourétes.
There, with many more beside,
I myself killed Íphiklos
and great Áphares, my mother's quick-fighting broth-
   ers. See you,
the war god, reckless in anger,
knows not friend from foe in the fighting.
Bolts are thrown blind from our hands
against the lives of all fighting against us,

and the flown spear brings death
to all against whom the god directs it.

The proud daughter of Thestios,
who (to my sorrow) was my mother,
did not take this into account,
but plotted my death. A pitiless woman she.
She took from its carven box
and broke and burned the log, soon gone,
which fate at my birth had designed
to be the measure of my own life,
lost with my death, I lost with it. I was then
in the very act of plundering
the strong body of Daípylos' son
Klýmenos, caught before the walls
where our enemies had fled away
to the ancient and strong-founded city

Pleuron. Little was the sweetness of life I had left
    then.
I felt the strength going from me,
ah, and with tears, in sorrow the last of my breathing,
the young force gone and the glory."
They say that Amphítryon's son
who never feared battlecry, then, that only time
felt eyes fill with tears, in pity
over that much-suffering man
and spoke to him in answer
thus: "Better for mortals never to come into existence,

never to look on the sun's shining.
Still, seeing there will be no advantage
got for us in mourning these matters,
we should put our minds to that which we may get done.
Could it be that within the halls
of Oíneus, the beloved of Ares,
there is among his unwedded daughters
one whose beauty is like your own?
Such a one I could wish to take as my shining bride."

To him now the spirit
of battle-brave Meleágros answered:
"I left behind in the house
Deïaneíra, her throat still green
with youth, and innocent still
of love, and the charms love can work on the flesh."

White-armed Lady of Legend, Kallíope,
bring to a halt your compact chariot
here. Sing Zeus, the son of Kronos,
Olympian god and lord of the gods on Olympos;
sing the unwearied surging river
Álpheos; sing the strength of Pelops;
Pisa the meadow where the glorious
horse Pherénikos won his race,
outfooting all, and back to the strong walls of Syracuse,
back to Híeron brought returning
the leafed branch of high success.
For grace and sake of truth it becomes us
to give praise, and with both hands push
rancorous spite away, when
any man does well and prospers.

Such was the gracious saying of the great Boiotian,
Hesiod, the close follower
of the Muses: "When the immortal gods set a man
    high,
let men's fame be given him also."
Lightly will I obey,
turn no inch from the course but let my lips' acclama-
    tion
be conveyed to Híeron. Thence
grow the stocks of excellent plants
which may Zeus, the great gardener,
keep in stillness of peace, untroubled forever.

4 · *Olympian Ode for Híeron* (*Chariot Race*)

Of Demeter, queen of most fruitful Sicily,
with her daughter, Maiden of the violet

garland, sing, Kleio, dispenser of sweetness,
sing for Olympic fields the speed of Híeron's

horses, who ran with towering success beside them;
with glory there beside the broad-whirling stream
of Álpheos they made Deinómenes' prospering
son the winner of garlands, and the uncounted

multitude cried in his honor:
"Ah, thrice fortunate this man
who from Zeus's own hand bestowed
with highest privilege of place
among Hellenes, knows how to keep his tower-piled
    wealth
clear of the hiding sheath of darkness."

Streets are alive with festal sacrifices
of oxen, alive with entertainment of friends
from far. High wrought and shining with gold, the
    gleam
plays from tripods set in a row before

the temple, where the greatest of groves is sacred
to Phoebus by the Kastalian stream, and men
of Delphoi served him. Let the God be glorified,
God, for over fortunes his power is greatest.

There was a time the lord of horse-taming
Lydia saw destined things
come to pass, saw Zeus's decree
fulfilled and brought to an end
when Sardeis fell to the horde of the Persians, only
Apollo, he of the golden sword,

guarded and kept him. Now Croesus came to the day
    of tears
unhoped for and had no mind to endure
slavery still, but let build a pyre
before the bronze-nailed wall of his courtyard

and there with his gracious wife ascended
and with his daughters of the braided hair, who wept

and mourned incessantly. Then Croesus lifted
his hands, and theirs, to the steep air

and spoke: "O powerful spirit,
where is the gratitude of gods?
Where is the king who is Leto's son?
The house of Alyáttes is fallen,
and nothing befalls me for all the thousand treasures
I had conveyed to him before,

no, but the aged citadel of the Lydians
burns, and Paktólos' gold-spinning waters
run red with blood, our wives are led forth
from their strong secret houses in shame.

All that I hated before is sweet now. Best to die."
So he spoke, and caused a soft-stepping attendant
to light the piled wood. The maidens his daughters
        broke out
in tears, and stretched their hands to their mother,

for to mortals the death seen coming
is bitterest of all ways to die.
But now, as the shining power
of the flames' menace burst high,
it was Zeus who drove a cloud's dark sheathing
above them and drenched the yellow flame.

Nothing passes belief when a god's intention
wills it. So Delian-born Apollo
carried off to the land of the Hyperboréans
the ancient, settled him there with his light-foot
        daughters, because

he was pious, because beyond all other
mortals he gave gifts to sacred Pytho.
So he. Of those now in Hellas, there is none,
O Híeron high in praise, who will venture

to say any man has given more
gold to Loxias than you. Therefore,
the man who fattens not on rancor
can readily speak praise of one

whom God loves, who loves horses, a man of battles,
who holds scepter from Zeus of the laws,

who holds place from the violet-wreathed Muses,
whose own hand was terrible once in war,
though now, in old age, you look on the day's blessing
quietly, and know it will not be long.

Still, hope is treacherous, she hides under the hearts
of us who are mortal. The lord of oracles,
Apollo, said to the son of Pheres:
"You are mortal. Best to have two predictions

in hand. Think to see tomorrow's
sun, and no sun thereafter.
Think to live for fifty years
through in deep-based wealth to the end.
Do your duties, so win your pleasure. Here lies
advantage higher than all."

I speak to one who can follow me. The deep
of the sky stains not. The water of the sea
is not dirtied with rot. Gold fights tarnish.
But it is not allowed for a man to pass

where age is gray, and then once more recover
strong youth. Yet there is no diminution
in man's good, his light, as the body goes. Still
the Muse sustains him. Híeron, you have shown out

the greatest splendors in flowers of wealth
before men. If one does well,
not silence brings his appropriate
glory. And with his honors here remembered,
men shall sound out too the exquisite grace
of me, the nightingale of Keos.

5 · *Pythian Ode for Alexidámos of Metapóntion* (*Wrestling*)

Victory, O sweet-giver,
on you your father, throned aloft
among Uranians granted

high place, and on golden Olympos
standing close beside Zeus,
you help ordain the end
on mortal and immortal endeavors:
be kind, O daughter of deep-haired
Styx who decrees the right: since it is by you
that now Metapóntion, city
prized by the gods, is held
by the revels and festivity of strong-limbed young men,
and they sing the Pythionician
glorious young sons of Phaískos.

With gentle eyes the Delian-
born son of Leto the deep-girdled
glanced upon him; and many
the wreaths of flowers on Alexidámos
were tossed there in the plain
of Kirrha, for grace of his powerful
all-overcoming wrestling.
The sun upon all that day
never once saw him thrown to the ground. Also
I will say that in the sacrosanct
levels of holy Pelops
beside where Álpheos runs in his beauty, had not some one
twisted justice away from a straight course,
with green olive of the all-friendships

wreathing his hair he had come
back to the herd-pasturing plain and to his own country.
It was no competitor
who by subtle shifts of his skill
brought the boy down in this sweet-spaced country,
but either some god was to blame,
or else the much-faltering judgments of mortals
took the uttermost glory out of his hands.
Now Artemis of the Wilds,
she of the golden distaff, she
of the bow-glory, kind, brought him shining
victory, she to whom on a day

Abas' son and his sweet-robed daughters
founded an altar of many prayers.

These daughters the queen almighty Hera
drove in rout from the lovely halls
of Proitos, with overmastering force
binding their hearts to madness. They
still in their girls' youth of heart
had visited the temple-precinct
of the goddess girt in robes of sea-dyes,
and boasted their father by far
for wealth overpassed the fair goddess throned
by the side of august powerful
Zeus; and the goddess in her rage
forced into their breasts back-eddying thoughts,
and they fled away to the leafy mountains,
crying in voices of horror

leaving behind the city of Tiryns
and the streets built by the gods.
For now it was the tenth year
that, abandoning god-favored Argos,
these brazen-shielded demigods, who
feared no battlecry, had been dwelling
there with their king, the much-admired.
There had been flame-ravening quarrel,
upsprung from some flimsy beginning, between
Proitos and Akrísios, brothers,
and they piled their people with quarrels,
lawsuits without end, and disconsolate fighting,
till the people begged these sons of Abas
to divide the barley-laden land

fairly, and the younger should settle
Tiryns, before they headed into some feud beyond solving;
and Zeus son of Kronos, respecting
the line of Dánaos and horse-driving
Lýnkeus, consented to put
an end to their horrifying sorrows.
The monstrous Cyclópes arriving

labored them a handsome wall for their glorious
city, and there the godlike heroes
far renowned lived on, forsaking
Argos the acclaimed, the pasture of horses.
It was from Tiryns they fled,
in wild tumult, these unwedded
girls, the dark-haired daughters of Proitos.

And the sorrow closed on his heart
and a stranger-impulse struck upon him,
for he pondered in his heart
the driving-in of a double-edged dagger,
but his men at arms by his side
stood and with gentling words
and force of their hands restrained him.
Now for thirteen whole months
the daughters were roving wild in the shadowy forest
and fled up and down, through sheep-raising
Arkadia; but when at last
their father came to the sweet-running water of Lousos,
there he washed clean, and crying aloud
entreated her of the crimson veil,

the ox-eyed daughter of Leto
as he lifted his arms up into the shining
beams of the horse-fleet sun,
that she should lead him his children back
from their sorry perverted madness
"I will sacrifice you twenty oxen,
never broken, red-coated."
Then she of the noblest father,
lady of wild beasts, heard his prayer, and persuading Hera
set free the wild-flower-garlanded girls
from their godless insanity
They made her a holy precinct and altar
straightway, and stained it with blood of sheep,
and established dances of women.

From there, in the company

of Achaíans, warlike men, you have passed to a horse-
　　prospering
city, and under fortune now
abide in Metapóntion, O
golden lady of armies,
and have your delightful grove
by the clear water of Kasas, where champions
planted it for you when, in the fulness of time
and by ordinance of the blessed immortals
they sacked the strong-founded city
of Priam, they with the bronze-armored Atreídai. He
whose mind judges fairly will find
that in time complete, the Achaíans' deeds
of war are numbered in thousands.